DASH

Eric J. Aronson

DASH

ISBN: 978-0-9769490-4-6

Published by

a division of DASH Systems, LLC

PO Box 773
Syosset, NY 11791

Tel: 516.677.9111
Fax: 516.677.9110

E-mail: info@dashlive.com
Web: www.dashlive.com

For my four children…Johnny Boy, Sissy Ca, E.J., and Isabella, you are what makes my DASH worth living.

TABLE OF CONTENTS

PART FOUR – HAPPINESS

INTRODUCTION

When you die, there will be two dates on your tombstone: the date of your birth and the date of your death. Those two dates will be separated by a "dash" – and that dash will represent your life.

It's been said many times, but it bears repeating: "Life is short!" Even at its longest, a human life is but a blink of an eye in the face of eternity. Each of us would be considered extremely lucky to live even 100 years. But compare that number to the estimated age of the earth – 4 billion years. As you can see, the time we live on this planet will be insignificant.

However, this doesn't mean that our lives are insignificant. The worth of a human life doesn't depend upon its longevity. It depends upon what we do with the time we are allotted, no matter how long or short. It's the "dash" between the years that makes the difference.

History is filled with examples of men and women who have impacted the course of history during the course of their dash. Some of these people lived long and full lives like Winston Churchill, whose leadership of England during World War II was instrumental in preventing Hitler's domination of Europe. Churchill lived until he was 90 and proved to be one of the most influential people of the 20th century.

On the other hand, Dr. Martin Luther King died at age 39, but not before leading a civil rights movement that would do more for racial equality in just one decade than had been accomplished in the previous 90 years. In fact, some of history's greatest figures are men and women whose lives were all too brief. For instance, Joan of Arc didn't live to see her 20th birthday. And Mozart died at 35. Yet each of these people literally changed the course of history in their short dash through eternity.

In fact, arguably the single most influential person of the last two millennia only lived to the age of 33. Moreover, little is known of his life until the age of 30. However, millions of people are still talking about those last three years. Of course, the man to whom I'm referring is Jesus of Nazareth.

Now, I understand that not everyone is destined to go down in the annals of history. However, that doesn't mean we all can't play a role in history. For every hero in our history books, there are 100 who are unsung. An unsung hero taught Michelangelo how to hold a paint brush. An unsung hero taught Einstein how to perform basic arithmetic. An unsung hero taught Betsy Ross how to thread a needle. In fact, every person who has ever excelled at anything had a teacher or a mentor, and often several. The key to making the most of your dash may not be to influence millions of people around the world but rather to influence one person in *your* world.

There is a wonderful story of a man who was walking along a beach one morning. Every few steps, he would bend down, pick up a starfish, and throw it back into the ocean. A second man came upon the first and asked, "What are you doing?" "I am saving starfish," replied the first man. The second man became incredulous. "Are you kidding? If you spent all day and night tossing starfish back into the ocean, you could never save them all. There are too many of them! Besides, in the grand scheme of things, they are just starfish.

It doesn't matter if they live or die." In silence, the first man bent down, picked up another starfish and tossed it into the ocean. "It mattered to *that* one."

How you live your dash matters to the people with whom you come into contact. It matters to your spouse. It matters to your children. It matters to your co-workers and clients. It matters to the members of your church or social organization. The purpose of this book is to help you create as much meaning as possible out of your dash.

> **"Let us so live that when we come to die even the undertaker will be sorry."**
> – Mark Twain

THE RACE OF LIFE

In one sense, our dash through life is a lot like a race. At birth, we are lined up at the starting line. At first, we stumble out of the blocks, but before long we gradually pick up speed until we come to the first hurdle. It may be an illness or a learning disability or the divorce of our parents; it's different for each of us. Some of us sail over the first hurdle and continue on in our race at full stride. Some of us nick the first hurdle as we pass over it, slowing us down in the race. And others fall flat on their faces, suffering cuts, bruises or worse.

Regardless of what happens with that first hurdle, we must continue running the race. The race of life doesn't stop for anyone. This can be a disturbing fact, but it's true. We have all hit major life hurdles that have knocked us off our feet – the death of a loved one, a divorce, the loss of a job, bankruptcy, etc. During these times, it seems hard to imagine that life can go on, but it does. The sun rises the next day. People go to work. Couples get married and have babies. The race continues and so must each of us, even if we have to stagger, limp or crawl through the race to the next hurdle.

3

I hate to be the bearer of bad news, but your dash is going to be littered with hurdles. I suspect that this is something you've already discovered for yourself. There will always be things in life that will require you to adjust your stride and take a little extra effort to surmount. In fact, when you run out of hurdles, your dash is over and you are dead.

In this book, I will introduce you to the Dash Principles. These principles have been derived through years of extensive study, through my own life experiences and through those of my clients. Many of these principles were first introduced thousands of years ago by Socrates, Buddha, Confucius and others, and have withstood the test of time. These principles will not remove the hurdles from your life but they will allow you to clear more of them and recover more quickly when you do hit them.

THE DASH PRINCIPLES

In this book, I use the word "dash" as not only a metaphor for life but also as an acronym to help you get the most out of your life. DASH stands for Determination, Attitude, Success and Happiness. By DASHing your way through life, you can eliminate stress, enjoy inner peace, create fulfilling and long-lasting relationships, boost your creativity, make better decisions, enjoy better health, succeed in business, secure a promotion, meet the perfect person and generally take charge of your life.

Determination

Everything in life begins with making a decision. Regardless of whether that decision is to go back to school, save for your child's college education or scale Mt. Everest, the starting point is a decision. However, it doesn't end with a decision.

For instance, if five birds are sitting on a wire and one of them decides to fly away, how many are still left? The answer is all five of them are still sitting on the wire. One bird's "decision" to fly away did not remove it from the wire. In fact, we all know people just like this bird, who continually "decide" (usually on New Year's Eve) to become more involved in church, lose weight or quit smoking. Yet they do nothing to turn their decisions into action.

It takes more than a decision to change your life: it requires **determination**. In the first part of this book, I'll not only help you decide how you will spend your dash, but I'll also help you act accordingly. Once you become determined to create a certain reality, you will find yourself literally drawn toward its achievement.

> **"Definiteness of purpose is the starting point of all achievement."**
> —**W. Clement Stone**

Attitude

However, determination is the just the first part of the DASH System. The second part is developing the proper mental **attitude**. It's been said that nothing can stop the person with the right mental attitude from achieving goals and nothing on earth can help the person with the wrong mental attitude. In the second part of this book, I will share with you the attitudes that will help you make the most out of your dash.

Success

In the third part of this book, I will share with you the traits of people who have achieved **success**. Of course, we all have our own unique definition of what "success" means. Some of us believe success is a big home, a fancy car and lots of money. Others believe success is a happy home life. And still others believe that success is starting a business or founding a charitable organization. Nevertheless, I believe that the success we are all seeking was best described by Robert Louis Stevenson:

"The man is a success who has lived well, laughed often and loved much; who has gained the respect of intelligent men and the love of children; who has filled his niche and accomplished his task; who leaves the world better than he found it, whether by an improved poppy, a perfect poem or a rescued soul; who never lacked appreciation of earth's beauty or failed to express it; who looked for the best in others and gave the best he had."

If you are looking to accomplish any (or preferably all) of these things, then there are certain success traits you'll need to learn. Regardless of the chosen field, successful people share common traits. By incorporating these traits into your daily actions, you can achieve greater levels of success in your life, too.

Happiness

The final letter in DASH stands for **happiness**. Unfortunately, many of us mistakenly believe that success is synonymous with happiness. We think that once we become successful, we will automatically be happy. Sadly, this is not always true. The world is filled with examples of "highly successful" individuals who do not lead happy lives. The fact is that no amount of material or financial success will ever be enough to compensate for poor peace of mind, poor health or poor family relationships.

In my view, happiness comes from achieving balance in life. The key is to balance your health, family, friendships, career and spirituality in such a way so they support your dash. The DASH System is not so much a success program as it is a LIFE program. Therefore, the final section of the book is dedicated to teaching you how to be happy so that you may be successful – and not the other way around.

Part One

DETERMINATION

"Determination is a power that exists and only becomes available when you know exactly what you want and do not stop until you achieve it."

—Eric J. Aronson

CHAPTER 1

The Buffet of Life

Recently, while eating at a buffet restaurant, I was struck by the similarities between the buffet and life itself. At a buffet, you are presented with an almost unlimited variety of choices. In fact, there are usually far more food items than you could ever consume in 10 meals. Life is the same way. You can't experience all the things life has to offer in 10 lifetimes.

In life, like a buffet, you have to make choices. You simply can't have, do, see or be everything that is available to you. Your "plate" can only hold so much. So how do you decide what to put on your plate? Well, some people never seem to decide. We've all seen them wandering aimlessly around the buffet, going from station to station but never putting anything on their plates. These people are like mosquitoes in a nudist camp – they see lots of opportunity, but can't decide where to start.

The rest of us seem to make our choices in one of two ways. Some of us get in a line and just start selecting items until our plates are full. This is the easiest way to get through a buffet line – or through life, for that matter. The problem with this approach is that you wind up with some things on your plate that you don't enjoy.

In my view, the better way to make your way through the buffet of life is to go from station to station, only choosing those things that you *really* enjoy. Of course, this requires more work because seldom are all of your favorites at the same station. Moreover, this requires patience because the lines are usually longer for the popular items. Nevertheless, making the extra effort makes the difference between being merely full and being *fulfilled.*

THE TALE OF TWO MEN

To better illustrate the difference between these two approaches, here are two true stories about two men. The first involves a man for whom nothing ever seemed to go right. It started when he was a child. As a hyperactive boy, he was always getting into trouble. At the age of 6, his parents took him to see a therapist. Unfortunately, the therapist they chose began sexually abusing the young boy.

The boy reported the abuse to his parents, who unfortunately thought it to be another of the boy's schemes – and the abuse continued for years. At age 13, the boy suffered another blow when his mother died of cancer. His father remarried, and the boy went through the uncomfortable process of fitting a new stepfamily into an already chaotic life. He struggled his way through adolescence, earning the distinction in high school as being the "most likely not to succeed." And this "honor" was bestowed upon him by none other than his guidance counselor.

As is often the case, this boy lived up to the expectations placed upon him. As an adult, he bounced from job to job. Eventually he was convicted of a felony and was sent to prison. Isolated from friends and loved ones, he sank into depression.

The second man was a stockbroker. After working at a

couple of brokerage firms, he decided to start his own firm. Within two years, he transformed a modest investment into *millions*. Later, he founded a company that helped develop much of the global positioning satellite technology used in today's automobiles. Then he went on to create the one of the largest bartering Web sites on the Internet.

He also met the woman of his dreams, got married and had four beautiful children. He bought a mansion and drove luxury automobiles. He participated in charity events, which brought him face to face with giants in business and entertainment. In short, he had a wonderful life.

Both stories are true and involve people I know personally. Sometimes I wonder how two lives could have turned out so differently. This is particularly true because both lives involve the same person – ME. Yes, I am the man in both stories. I was troubled, abused and eventually incarcerated. I am also a man who has amassed a considerable fortune, a wonderful family, and has helped others do the same thing.

DETERMINATION

As I said, I have often wondered what has made the difference in my life. How could I have come so far? What has accounted for the radical reversals of fortune in my life? I honestly believe the answer comes down to one word – **determination.**

As long as I was willing to float through life, taking my cues from others, I was subject to abuse, criticism, betrayal and a host of other problems. In short, I was like the person in the buffet line, who dutifully follows the person in front of him, indiscriminately heaping food on his plate. Eventually I got to the point where my plate was full of stuff, much of which I found distasteful. The old saying is really true: "If you don't stand for something, you'll fall for anything." I fell for abuse. I fell for low expectations. I fell for quick schemes that landed me in prison.

However, when I took the time to look around from station to station to **decide** how I would fill my plate, things changed dramatically. I was able to create three multimillion dollar businesses in less than five years by choosing a better course. None of these businesses simply dropped into my lap. Instead, in each case, I had to leave the line I was in and search out a new opportunity.

There is a story of a man who was driving through the Black Hills near Mount Rushmore when he ran into a snowstorm. He soon lost all sense of direction but, as luck would have it, he came up behind a snowplow. Relieved, he kept as close to the snowplow as possible for what seemed like hours.

Finally, the plow stopped and the driver came over to the man and asked, "Where are you headed?" The man replied, "I'm on my way to Montana." The snowplow driver laughed and said, "Well, you'll never get there following me. I'm plowing out this parking lot!" This happens to many of us in life. We blindly follow the path of a parent or older brother or respected colleague, only to find ourselves traveling in circles. This has certainly been true in my life.

Please know that the stories of my successes are not meant to impress you, but rather impress *upon you* the importance of choosing your course in life, as opposed to just going with the flow. When I have failed in life, it has been for lack of purpose, and when I have succeeded, it has been because I knew what I wanted and why. The next few chapters are dedicated to helping you do just that.

Go For The Great!

In one of the classic episodes of I *Love Lucy*, Lucy and Ethel take jobs in a chocolate factory. They are assigned the task of wrapping up little pieces of chocolate as they travel along a conveyor belt. At first, they find the task easy to perform. However, before long, the conveyor belt speeds up and the two women find themselves in an impossible situation. They simply cannot keep up with the constant flow of chocolate. In a noble (not to mention hilarious) effort to prevent unwrapped chocolate from reaching the next level of production, they start stuffing chocolate into their mouths, into their hats, and even down their shirts. However, they were fighting a losing battle and eventually, they lost the war. At the end of the day, they were stuffed with chocolate, fatigued, and yes, unemployed.

As we excitedly DASH into this New Year, we need to be careful to avoid Lucy and Ethel's predicament. Often, when we first get involved with a new project or organization, the pace starts out at a manageable speed. However, as our skills and confidence increase, life has a way of speeding up the conveyor belt. Soon, there are more demands on our time and resources. In fact, you may be already experiencing this phenomenon in your job, business, civic, or other organization. The trick is to find a way to enjoy the bounty of "goodies" flowing your way without becoming overwhelmed in the process.

Your first thought may be to try to slow down the conveyor belt. However, the truth of the matter is that the conveyor belt of life does not slow down for *anyone*. Opportunities don't wait just because you aren't ready for them. They simply present themselves, and if you aren't ready to tackle them, they will seek out someone who is ready.

Therefore, you must learn to be choosy about picking your projects. After all, Lucy and Ethel would have been much better off if they had tried to wrap just one out of every ten chocolates that came whizzing past. Instead, they tried to wrap them all and ended up in total failure. Remember, it's better to complete just one project successfully than it is to leave 100 projects half done. When you take on too many projects, you run the real risk of pleasing no one (including yourself).

The better solution is to pick and choose those projects that offer the greatest value to you. For instance, let's suppose you are seated in front a conveyor belt that is carrying coins instead of chocolate. You can keep all the money that you can grab, but sadly the conveyor belt is moving too fast for you to be able to grab all the coins. In this case, you have two choices: (1) you can just grab coins indiscriminately, trying to obtain as many coins as possible; or (2) you can make an effort to grab only the larger coins. As you can guess, the first strategy will lead to you obtaining the greatest *quantity* of coins, but the second strategy will lead to you obtaining the greatest *value* of coins.

Which of these two strategies are you using to deal with the opportunities that are flowing into your life? Are you just taking opportunities as they come along, or are you being discriminate and only pursuing those projects that offer the greatest value to you? And please don't think that when I use the word "value" that I'm only referring to monetary value. There are many forms of value— physical health, harmonious relationships, spiritual development, etc. And your best chance of obtaining these higher values is to develop the discipline to let go of the lesser values.

As Kenny Rogers once said, "Don't be afraid to give up the good to go for the great."

THOUGHTS FOR YOUR DASH

Determination

"The men who succeed are the efficient few. They are the few who have the ambition and will power to develop themselves."

HERBERT N. CASSON

Attitude

"He is rich or poor according to what he is, not according to what he has."

HENRY WARD BEECHER

Success

"Those who attain to any excellence commonly spend life in some single pursuit, for excellence is not often gained upon easier terms."

SAMUEL JOHNSON

Happiness

"Treasure the love you receive above all. It will survive long after your gold and good health have vanished."

OG MANDINO

CHAPTER 2

Destiny is a Decision

As I see it, your dash is about two things: being and doing. How are you going to *be* as a human being? And what are you going to *do* or contribute?

Most of us believe that we could do more with our dash but feel limited and overwhelmed by our situation, by the demands that burden us and by our own fears. So how do we find meaning in our lives? How do we find a way to make a difference that matters to each of us?

MAKE A DECISION

The answer to this last question is amazingly simple: we must simply *decide*. As William Jennings Bryan said, "Destiny is not a matter of chance, it is a matter of choice." You must consciously decide what you want your dash to be about. Make a conscious decision about your purpose in life. Take a moment to consider some of the greatest events in history. You'll find that they all started with something as simple as a decision.

On August 2, 1492, Christopher Columbus **decided** to prove once and for all that the world was round by setting sail for the New World. On July 4, 1776, 56 men gathered in Philadelphia **decided** they were not willing to live under the tyranny of British rule and signed the Declaration of Independance. On September 22, 1862, Abraham Lincoln **decided** to end the shameful practice of slavery by issuing the Emancipation Proclamation. On December 17, 1903, Orville and Wilbur Wright **decided** to prove the experts wrong by making the first successful flight of a heavier-than-air flying machine. On December 1, 1955, Rosa Parks **decided** she would take a stand against injustice by refusing to give up her seat on a bus in Montgomery, Alabama.

Of course, these are a few of the thousands of people throughout history who made important decisions. But none of these decisions would have meant anything unless they were backed by action. For instance, the frustration and agitation of our founding fathers would not have made them free had they simply sat in a room in Independance Hall and complained about it. Instead, they took action. They made a declaration that changed the course of history.

Today can be another important day in history. Today you can make a decision about how you will spend your dash. And you don't need to sail across the ocean or fly off a cliff to do it. You simply need to make the decision that you *will* make a certain thing happen. You don't need to know how you are going to do it, but you must know that you *will* do it. Once you get this kind of blinding determination working for you, failure is not an option. You will either succeed or die trying.

This may sound somewhat dire, but life is serious business. As far as we know, we only get one shot at this thing called "life." We are allotted a short period of time in which to make our mark on the world. And the chance of any of us "stumbling" onto our greatness is extremely small. If we want to bring about a certain reality, then we must be **determined** to make it happen.

18

In his first address to the House of Commons as Prime Minister, Winston Churchill said, "You ask, 'What is our aim?' I can answer in one word: 'Victory!' Victory at all costs, victory in spite of terror, victory however long and hard the road may be; for without victory there is no survival."

Churchill made it clear to the world that his people would do everything in their power to repel the assault of Hitler. With the advantage of hindsight, it seems pretty clear that Hitler should have aborted his plans for world domination at that point. So long as the people of Great Britain were determined to remain free, they could never be conquered.

"Nothing can resist the human will that will stake even its existence on its stated purpose."
—Benjamin Disraeli

FIND YOUR PURPOSE

Your mission in life probably isn't so dire, but there is *something* for you to do. There is some contribution that only you can make. There is some purpose for your dash – a reason why you are on this planet at this time. Ask yourself, "What will go on my tombstone besides the dates?" What words will people use to describe your dash? Remember, everyone gets a dash regardless of whether their journey through life was meaningful, meaningless or even malicious. The key is to decide what that purpose is and to make a plan to fulfill it.

There is great power in decision. Once you decide your purpose in life, you will no longer struggle to do the things you feel you must. The need for discipline will be a thing of the past. This is not because you won't need discipline to achieve your purpose but rather because you will no longer struggle with discipline. You will be almost effortlessly drawn toward those activities that help you accomplish your mission.

W. Clement Stone put it this way: "When you discover

your mission, you will feel its demand. It will fill you with enthusiasm and a burning desire to get to work on it."

Someone once asked the great humorist H. L. Mencken why he continued to work into his old age. Mencken replied, "I keep on working for the same reason that a chicken continues to lay eggs." In other words, he continued to work because there was something in him that he *had* to get out. Each of us should attempt to find this type of "calling."

THE POWER OF FOCUS

Purpose truly is power. In fact, having a focus is often the difference between success and failure. In some contexts, it can mean the difference between life and death. For instance, let's suppose you are marooned on a deserted island and need to start a fire. Unfortunately, you don't have any matches. However, you do have a magnifying glass and the power of the sun available to you. If you gather some dried leaves together, can you start a fire with the magnifying glass? The answer is "yes," but only if you *focus* the power of the sun by holding the magnifying glass in one place. You can't start a fire by moving the magnifying glass back and forth across the leaves. Likewise, you can't burn your place into history by moving back and forth from activity to activity.

The laser beam is the perfect illustration of this principle. A laser beam can cut through steel but only because it is tightly focused. On the other hand, the same amount of light shown through a flashlight wouldn't even slice through a stick of butter. The sole source of a laser's power is in its focus. The same is true for you. When you become focused on an outcome, you can move through all types of obstacles.

FOLLOW YOUR BLISS

You might agree with what I've said, but still don't know how to select a purpose. Remember, life is a buffet with an unlimited number of choices. So how do you decide amongst the multitude of choices available to you? The answer is to follow your bliss. As Naomi Stephen writes in *Finding Your Life's Mission:* "Your mission will manifest in you when you decide to listen to your heart's desire."

Ask yourself, "What do I love to do more than anything? What could I do all day, everyday?" Sometimes when I ask this question in private coaching sessions, my clients will respond by saying that they like sex or cheesecake more than anything. However, after some laughter and joking, I'm able to get them thinking about other forms of happiness, because the truth is that I have yet to meet the person who could make love or eat cheesecake all day, every day. And quite frankly, I'm not sure I want to meet that person either!

Your true bliss is the activity (or activities) that you look forward to doing and, no matter how often you do it, you just can't seem to get enough of it. For some people, their bliss is art or poetry. Whenever they have a free moment, they are drawing or writing. Others enjoy gardening or home improvement projects. On Friday afternoon, when most people are just looking forward to a relaxing weekend, these folks are planning where they will plant the squash or trying to determine how many buckets it will take to paint the fence again. What are you looking forward to doing next?

Your Best Chance for Success

One of the key advantages to following your bliss is that it increases your chances of accomplishing your purpose. Crossing the gap between where you are now and where you want to be will require some refinement and

21

enhancement of your God-given talents. This is a fancy way of saying that you will need to practice your craft. If you choose a craft that you enjoy, you are far more likely to put in the time necessary to improve your skills. As noted speaker Glenn Van Ekeren says, "To be considered accomplished in any area is the result of taking even the smallest talent and practicing it into excellence."

Take the story of Minnesota Twins pitcher Jim Kaat. Over the course of his career, he was one of the best left-handed pitchers in the American League. He traced much of his success to Johnny Sain, a pitching coach hired by the Twins in 1966.

Shortly after assuming his coaching position, Sain called Kaat into his office and asked, "Jim, what are your four best pitches?" Kaat responded, "My fastball is my best pitch. Then comes my curve, my slider and my change-up." Sain then asked, "Which pitch do you spend the most time practicing?" "My slider and change-up," Kaat replied. "If I can improve on those two pitches, I know I'll have a great season." Sain hesitated and then said, "Jim, I see things a little differently and I want you to take a different approach. Work on your fastball. Work on it during practice and warm-ups and throw your fastball 80 to 90 percent of the time. You'll win a lot of ballgames."

Kaat admits that this was not the "sage" advice he was looking for. Nevertheless, he decided to follow Sain's advice anyway. The result was that Kaat won 26 games in 1966 and was awarded the American League's Cy Young award, the award given to the best pitcher in the league.

Often, we spend much of our time trying to overcome our limitations. We spend hour after hour working on our "sliders" and "change-ups," which never seem to improve. This is unfortunate considering that each of us has a "fastball" – some talent or skill that we can perform almost effortlessly. Also, in almost all cases, it's one of the things that we love to do (perhaps because it's so effortless).

I used my fastball to create miracles in the brokerage business. My fastball is my ability to motivate others to take action. In just three years, I was able to motivate our sales-people to create incredible results for the firm and, more importantly, for themselves. One of my proudest accomplishments is that many people left my firm as millionaires.

However, none of this would have been possible had I used my time working on my weak areas. As you may know, the brokerage business is highly regulated and requires a tremendous amount of paperwork. Spending hour after hour filling out forms and setting up compliance procedures is not one of my top 10 favorite things to do. In fact, it probably doesn't even make the top 10,000.

So, I hired others to handle these tasks for me: people for whom paperwork was their fastball. They not only enjoyed the work more than I did, but they were better at it. This allowed me to use my fastball, and together we produced incredible results.

Your Greatest Joy

Another key advantage to following your bliss is that it adds to your happiness. When you align your purpose to your bliss, you can effortlessly do what you *should* do because it's also what you *want* to do. The most success-ful people in every field are those who love what they do. The best doctors are those who love the practice of medicine. On their vacations, you will find them sneak-ing away to steal a few minutes alone with a back issue of the Journal of the American Medical Association. The same holds true for all top professionals. Their friends and loved ones have to drag them away from their work.

Of course, I'm not suggesting that you become a "workaholic" or obsessed with your job. However, I am suggesting that in deciding how you will spend your dash, you take into account what you like to do. It can make the difference between a life of work and a life of play.

> **"We are not sent into the world to do anything into which we cannot put our hearts."**
> **—John Ruskin**

Your Highest Income

The third advantage to pursuing your passion is that it pays better. In *Getting Rich Your Own Way*, Srully Blotnick points to a study in which 1,500 young people were divided into two groups. Group A consisted of people who were embarking on a career for the money. Group B consisted of people who chose a career that they loved to do. Sadly, the number of people in Group A outnumbered the people in Group B by a margin of 5–1.

Researchers followed these two groups for 20 years. At the end of 20 years, 101 of the 1,500 participants were millionaires. However, the amazing thing is that all but one of the millionaires came from Group B. Just think, only 1 out of 1,250 people from Group A became wealthy, even though all of them made money pursuing their primary career objective. Yet 100 of the 250 from Group B became wealthy by simply pursuing what made them happy.

I suggest that you take a few moments to get clear on (1) your core values, and (2) your favorite activities. Remember, to give the greatest meaning to your dash, you must find a purpose. And the purpose that will give special meaning to your life will combine your values and your bliss. In Chapter 3, we will use this information to get a better picture of your purpose, but for now, simply spend time deciding what is important to you. Remember, the key to becoming and doing more is to decide.

Follow Your Nose

One of my favorite things to do is to sit down with my wife and children and watch classic Christmas tales like *Santa Claus is Coming to Town* and *Frosty the Snowman*. My all-time favorite Christmas tale is the story of *Rudolph the Red-Nosed Reindeer*. Perhaps, it's because I relate so well with Rudolph. As you remember, Rudolph was different from the other reindeer. He was born with a shiny nose (some would even say it glowed). As a result, he was called names and not allowed to play in any reindeer games.

Have you ever felt like Rudolph? I know I have. As a child, I was hyperactive and labeled a "bad kid." As a result, I missed my fair share of "reindeer games" sitting in the principal's office. Is there something about you that makes you like Rudolph? Perhaps, you don't look like everyone else. Or perhaps, you speak a little differently or walk funny. Or perhaps, you just see the world in a different light. You're not "hip" or "with it." You don't wear the "right" clothes, listen to the "right" music, or drive the "right" car.

If so, you should get excited because this difference could change your destiny. As you probably remember, one foggy Christmas Eve, Rudolph went from being ridiculed to being revered. But how did Rudolph finally find success? Did he have plastic surgery to "fix" his nose? Of course not! Rudolph was able to "go down in history" because of his nose, not in spite of it. Rudolph's glowing red nose turned out to be his greatest asset.

I relate to this story so well because I have been able to find success by following my nose. My "nose" is having high energy and not being able to take "no" for an answer. These qualities were troublesome as a child but they have proven themselves invaluable to my success as an entrepreneur. These qualities have helped me to create four successful businesses and amass a fortune for myself and others. In fact, upon closer look, I realize that my "big red nose" is my greatest asset. And so is yours.

For instance, your creativity may have caused others to label you as "weird" in the past, but it will be your creativity that will make others stand and cheer in the future. Likewise, your analytical nature may have caused others to view you as a "geek" or a "nerd", but that same skill is the one that could help you to create a multibillion-dollar software company (how many of us would kill to be as "nerdy" as Bill Gates or Steven Jobs?).

However, if you are going to sail off into your destiny, you must learn Rudolph's greatest skill—his humility. Just think, Rudolph had been teased and tormented mercilessly by the denizens of the North Pole. It would have been easy for him to reply to Santa's request to pull the sleigh by saying, "No way fat boy: you pull your own sleigh and I hope you run into a telephone pole on your trip!"

Although it might have been satisfying for Rudolph to give Santa and the other reindeer a taste of their own medicine, Rudolph would have been the one left with a bad taste in his mouth. To my knowledge, that one foggy Christmas Eve was Rudolph's only chance to shine. If Rudolph had let his ego get in the way, he would have missed his date with destiny.

Someday soon (I'd guess sooner than you think), the weather is going to get foggy and your detractors are going to need that special light you possess. Don't blow it by being bitter. Just remember what Frank Sinatra once said, "The best revenge is massive success."

"The hardest struggle of all is to be something different from what the average man is."

Charles M. Schwab

THOUGHTS FOR YOUR DASH

Determination
>"Do not go where the path may lead, go instead where there is no path and leave a trail."
> RALPH WALDO EMERSON

Attitude
>"An adventure is only an inconvenience rightly considered. An inconvenience is only an adventure wrongly considered."
> G. K. CHESTERTON

Success
>"You can accomplish by kindness what you cannot by force."
> PUBLILIUS SYRUS

Happiness
>"A cloudy day is no match for a sunny disposition."
> WILLIAM ARTHUR WARD

CHAPTER 3

Meet the Most Remarkable Person on Earth ... YOU!

After examining their values and passions, most of my clients are amazed at how much they learn about themselves. You probably had the same experience. In fact, although I've gone through this process a number of times myself, I still get something new out of it *every* time.

It's so easy to get caught up in getting the kids off to school, hustling off to work, fighting traffic on the way home, cooking dinner, and trying to get the kids to bed that we simply lose sight of ourselves and what's important to us. In short, we get so caught up in living our roles that we forget to direct the play.

This certainly happened to me. I became so caught up in the day-to-day struggles of life that I lost sight of the big picture and it almost cost me everything. Interestingly, it was at that point when life gave me the ultimate "timeout" – a chance to evaluate my life and priorities. Fortunately, life doesn't have to deliver such a drastic wakeup call because this is something you can do at any time.

THE BIG PICTURE

We all change over time. However, the changes are so slow and gradual that we don't seem to realize they've happened. It's like when your children are growing up. You often don't notice how big they're getting until a relative or friend points it out. Of course, this is only natural, but there are times when a lack of perspective can be dangerous.

For instance, have you ever gone swimming or bodysurfing at the beach? If so, then you know how easy it is to get swept down the beach with the current. From your perspective, you are simply going back and forth in a straight line, riding the waves and having a great time. However, you are also being moved, imperceptibly, along with the current. By the time you emerge from the water, you are a hundred yards or more from where you started.

This is what happens to many of us in life. We start moving back and forth in the current of life – riding the wave of success and failure. And then one day, we look around to see where we are and realize that we have drifted far off course – far from our core values and beliefs. This is why it's so important to get a "check-up from the neck-up" every so often.

> **"There is a time when we must firmly choose the course we will follow, or the relentless drift of events will make the decision."**
> **—Herbert V. Prochnow**

This is particularly true in the context of a marriage. You can become so busy working, driving the kids to soccer practice and picking up the dry cleaning, until one day you wake up and realize that you are sleeping next to a complete stranger. You don't share any hobbies, activities or common interests. When some couples are asked why they divorced, they say things like "we simply drifted apart." This is why it's not only important to check up on your core values and beliefs, but also those of your loved ones to make sure that your relationships don't get swept away in the currents of life.

GETTING BACK ON TRACK

Now, if you are like most people, you've probably drifted down the beach a little ways. For instance, one of your values may be adventure, but your life has started to settle into a routine. If that's the case, then it's not time to panic. Nor do you need to sell your house and travel through Europe on a moped. You simply need to take notice of the situation and make small adjustments. For instance, you could try driving a different route to work or eating at an Ethiopian restaurant or ordering a single latte instead of a double latte. The point is not to turn your life upside-down, but rather to reconnect with what's important to you.

The same thing is true if you notice that you have been neglecting one of your passions in life. For instance, let's suppose you really enjoy playing the piano but you haven't played in so long that you probably couldn't even find Middle C anymore. If that's the case, then take some time to clear away some of the junk that has accumulated on your piano and spend a few minutes each day playing. You will be amazed by how much light you can add to your life by simply following your bliss.

THE ONE AND ONLY YOU

You are the most remarkable person on this planet. And I mean it! Do you realize that of all of the billions of people who have lived before you and of all of the billions who will come after you, *none* of them was just like you? You are an original. Nietzsche described you as "a unique being, only once on this earth; and by no extraordinary chance will ever such a marvelously, picturesque piece of diversity in unity be put together a second time."

The Winning Lottery Ticket

On December 25, 2002, a West Virginia man won $317 million in the Powerball lottery. The odds of winning this lottery are just over 120 million to 1. Those are pretty steep odds. However, winning the lottery is a piece of cake in comparison to the odds of *you* being born in the first place.

You are the product of 23 chromosomes from your mother and 23 chromosomes from your father. Geneticists have determined that the odds of your parents having another child just like you are 10 to the 2 *billionth* power to 1. This number is so large that it's almost beyond our comprehension. In fact, it would take you 75 years working day and night just to write out this number by hand. The bottom line is that there will never be another you. You are truly a one-of-a-kind.

> **"Believe it, you are a real find, a joy in someone's heart. You are a jewel, unique and priceless. God don't make no junk!"**
> **—Herbert Banks**

Your Million Dollar Body

As a result, you are extremely valuable. A rare diamond or ruby can fetch millions at auction and, in the end, it's simply a rock – an unthinking, unfeeling, inanimate object. However, as a human being, you are so much more. You have the power to create miracles. Moreover, you are every bit as rare as the most perfect diamond. In short, you are priceless.

To put a price tag on your worth, let's look at a sample state worker's compensation table:

Body Part	Value
Loss of thumb	$60,000
Loss of first finger	$35,000
Loss of second finger	$30,000
Loss of third finger	$25,000
Loss of fourth finger	$20,000
Loss of hand	$190,000
Loss of arm	$250,000
Loss of great toe	$40,000
Loss of any other toe	$15,000
Loss of foot	$150,000
Loss of leg	$220,000
Loss of eye	$140,000
Loss of hearing in one ear	$50,000
Loss of hearing in both ears	$175,000
Permanent disfigurement, face or head	$150,000
Body as a whole/industrial disability	$500,000

As you can see from this chart, each of your arms is worth $250,000. Your legs are worth $220,000 apiece. Your eyes are worth $140,000 each and both ears are worth $175,000. If we throw in $150,000 for your face, then the total worth of your body is $1,545,000 – and that doesn't include your internal organs.

I'll admit this is a ghoulish way to look at the worth of a human being, but it makes a good point. Think about it. Do you treat your body like a million-dollar investment? For instance, if you had a million-dollar racehorse, would you feed it chocolate, let it drink wine or smoke cigarettes? It's just something to think about.

Your Billion-Dollar Mind

But we have totally neglected the most valuable part of you – your mind. While you possess a million dollar body, your mind is worth *billions*. In the summer of 2001, IBM built the ACSI White supercomputer for $110 million. This computer is capable of computing 12.3 trillion operations per second. Not bad, huh? Well, compared to the human brain, the ACSI White is an abacus. The human brain is capable of computing 10,000 trillion operations per second. In other words, IBM spent $110 million to build a computer that is several hundred times slower than your brain. Imagine how much IBM would have been willing to spend for your brain.

> **"Tis the mind that makes the body rich."**
> **—William Shakespeare**

Sadly, I suspect that most of us don't realize the enormous value within. I have to admit that for years I didn't realize it either. I would have never fed my body junk food if I had realized its value. And I definitely wouldn't have fed my mind with garbage. I let the negative experiences of my childhood warp my sense of value and worth.

YOUR PERMANENT GREATNESS

However, the truth of the matter is that no matter what happens to you, it doesn't diminish your value. For instance, let's suppose a stranger walked up to you holding a $100 bill in his hand and asked, "Who would like this $100 bill?" Would you want it? What if he then crumpled up the bill in his fist? Would you still want it? What if he then dropped the bill and started grinding it into the ground with his shoe? Would you still want it? Of course!

This is because crumpling, dropping or stomping on a $100 bill does not decrease its value. The same is true for you. You may have been dropped or crumpled or even stomped on, but you are still every bit as valuable as the day you were born. Poverty does not lessen your value. Addiction does not lessen your value. Neither does prison, obesity, divorce or an unhappy childhood. Sure, you might be a little worn around the edges, dirty and wrinkled, but you are still priceless.

A Foundation for Greatness

In fact, if you put pain and rejection in their proper place, they can serve as a foundation for future success. Whenever someone builds a skyscraper, the first step is to dig a huge hole in the ground – the foundation. And the bigger the building, the deeper and wider the builders must dig. In some ways, human beings are similar. We often reach great heights only after sinking to great depths.

The actor James Earl Jones is a perfect example. Today he is nationally known for the richness and power of his voice. In fact, companies are willing to pay handsomely just to use his voice to announce their products. This is quite a remarkable achievement considering that, as a child, he stuttered so badly that he had to communicate using written notes. Undoubtedly, the voice that has taken James Earl Jones to the top of the mountain was developed in the valley.

Your Unlimited Potential

I've spent much of this chapter telling you how incredible you are for a reason. In the next chapter, we will put into action the first component of The DASH System: **determination.** It is your determination that will make the rest of the steps possible in your journey to create a meaningful dash. However, before getting to that point, I want to share the following story with you:

On a warm summer day, a man was fishing from the bank of a river with amazing success. As if by divine intervention, he was catching fish at will – big ones and little ones. Amazingly, the fisherman was throwing back the big fish and keeping the little ones. A passerby noticed this rather odd behavior and said to the fisherman, "I'm sorry to be the one to tell you this but you're doing it wrong! You're supposed to keep the big ones and throw back the little ones." The fisherman replied, "I suppose you're right but all I've got is this little itty bitty frying pan."

Many of us are just like this fisherman. We are throwing back big dreams and aspirations because we mistakenly believe that all we have are little itty bitty frying pans of potential. Nothing could be further from the truth. As Thomas Edison said, "If we all did the things that we are capable of, we would literally astound ourselves." Therefore, consider the possibility of astounding yourself.

If you expect anything less, you do a disservice to yourself. And, perhaps more importantly, you do a disservice to the rest of us. As we discussed earlier, there has never been another you. With no effort on your part, you were given a million dollar body and a billion dollar mind. Moreover, you were given a special set of skills, talents and abilities that will *never* be duplicated. If you fail to use these special gifts, not only do you cheat yourself and your creator but you also cheat the rest of us. We will be *permanently* deprived of the opportunity to benefit from the unique gifts that were bestowed only upon you.

What's in a Name? EVERYTHING!

This week, I want to discuss with you the most valuable asset you possess. And believe it or not, it's not your home, your business, or your 401(k) balance. These assets are merely possessions and as a result, they come and go. For instance, a fire could destroy your home or business and a bad investment could wipe out your 401(k) balance. However, your greatest asset is not a reflection of what you have but rather it is a reflection of who you *are*. Your greatest asset is your name, or more specifically, your reputation.

Perhaps, the most eloquent explanation of the value of your reputation comes from William Shakespeare in the play *Othello* when Iago says:

> *Good name in man and woman, dear my lord,*
> *Is the immediate jewel of their souls:*
> *Who steals my purse steals trash; 'tis something, nothing;*
> *'Twas mine, 'tis his, and has been slave to thousands;*
> *But he that filches from me my good name*
> *Robs me of that which not enriches him*
> *And makes me poor indeed.*

Now, you may be thinking that this sentiment may have been true in Elizabethan England but not in 21st century America. However, just the opposite is true. In our modern society, your name is even more important than ever. For most of us, our name is our primary source of spending power. When we want to pay our mortgage or our utility bills, what do we do? We sign our names to a check. When we want to buy a television or pay for our airline tickets, what do we do? We sign our names to a credit card receipt.

And what determines the size or quality of the television or vacation we can purchase? It is our reputation. Someone with a reputation for financial abundance and trustworthiness can acquire more goods and services than someone with a lesser reputation. In fact, a good reputation is worth far more than gold. For instance, let's suppose that you are looking to buy a million-dollar home. To qualify for the purchase of the home, you may only have to come up with $100,000 in cash. The bank will lend you the other 90 percent of the money on the basis of your credit report (i.e., your *reputation* for paying your debts). Just think about that for a moment. All of your hard work and effort to accumulate cash for the down payment is worth only 10 percent of what your name is worth. And, in fact, if your name is good enough, the bank will lend you the *entire* purchase price.

As you can see, a good reputation is far more valuable than stocks, bonds, and real estate. And just as with any other valuable, it must be protected. After all, if you have a nice car, you probably have an alarm system installed. The same is probably true of your home. Therefore, it only makes sense to ADT your reputation as well.

Sadly, this is one of the lessons in life that I had to learn the hard way. In the past, I was very careless with my reputation, much more careless than I would have ever been with, say, my Lamborghini. I would never have left my expensive sports car out all night with the doors unlocked and the windows rolled down. However, there were many times when I left the doors to my reputation wide open. I became involved with people and schemes that not only robbed me of three years of freedom but perhaps more importantly, my good name.

As I've said many times before, my biggest motivation for doing what I do now is to restore a good name for my children. I want my children to be able to proudly say that their name is "Aronson." And I'm sure you want the same thing for your children (except, of course, you want them to use your last name instead). Therefore, here are three ways to keep your reputation under lock and key.

Hide Your Jewels—If you had millions of dollars in jewels lying around inside your home, would you advertise that fact? Of course not. You would not want to make yourself an easy target for thieves to rob you. In the same way, you don't want to make yourself an easy target for people to rob you of your good reputation by trying to dazzle everyone with your brilliance. For this reason, whenever possible, you should *under promise* and *over deliver*. People will never trash your reputation for delivering more than you said you would.

Hold the Key—What do you think would happen to your car if you parked it in a parking lot with the keys in the ignition and the door unlocked? Someone would probably hop in and drive it all over town, getting parking tickets, having accidents, and generally causing mayhem, right? Well the same thing happens when you let others hold the keys to your reputation. Therefore, you must be careful to always be in the driver's seat when it comes to your reputation. Whenever your reputation is on the line, you must be the one responsible for completing what you've promised.

For instance, if your department is preparing a big report for the next board meeting, you are going to be the one held responsible if the report is late or filled with errors. The board isn't going to care that your secretary was having a bad day or that the guys in the mailroom mixed up the addresses. The success of the project will affect *your* reputation, and for that reason, you must ultimately be responsible for checking everyone's work or delegating the task to someone whose reputation is as good as you want your reputation to be.

Install a LoJack—The purpose of the LoJack system is to locate your car when it is stolen. Whenever a car is reported stolen, the LoJack system in the car is activated remotely. Small radio frequency transceivers then emit inaudible sounds, which can be picked up by devices installed in police cruisers. Well, on many occasions, your reputation will get away from you too. When this happens, people will emit *audible* sounds expressing their displeasure about your reputation. The key is to have a network of people tuned into this frequency who can pick up the distress signal and relay the message back to you. This will allow you to rectify the problem and salvage your reputation.

The most important thing is to *constantly* guard your reputation. As Socrates once said, "Regard your good name as the richest jewel you can possibly be possessed of—for credit is like fire; when once you have kindled it you may easily preserve it, but if you once extinguish it, you will find it an arduous task to rekindle it again."

THOUGHTS FOR YOUR DASH

Determination
> "If you limit your choices only to what seems possible or reasonable, you disconnect yourself from what you truly want, and all that is left is a compromise."
>
> ROBERT FRITZ

Attitude
> "I discovered I always have choices and sometimes it's only a choice of attitude."
>
> JUDITH M. KNOWLTON

Success
> "Character is like a tree and reputation like its shadow. The shadow is what we think of it; the tree is the real thing."
>
> ABRAHAM LINCOLN

Happiness
> "The foolish man seeks happiness in the distance, the wise grows it under his feet."
>
> JAMES OPPENHEIM

CHAPTER 4

Charting a Course

As we discussed in the last chapter, you are one of a kind and priceless. In recognition of this fact, I have designed the DASH System to be the ultimate roadmap to help you get the most meaning out of your dash. By following the DASH Principles, you can achieve any result you want in your life – financial independence, loving relationships with your family, the career of your dreams, social contributions – you name it. However, even the best roadmap is worthless unless you first know your destination.

> **"If we could first know where we are, and whither we are tending, we could then better judge what to do and how to do it."**
> **—Abraham Lincoln**

WHERE ARE YOU?

Of course, this is obvious. However, what may not be so obvious is that you also need to know your starting point. To illustrate, let's suppose you visit a brand new shopping mall.

You'd like to pick up something for a friend at Sears but you don't know where the Sears is in this particular mall. Therefore, you consult the directory:

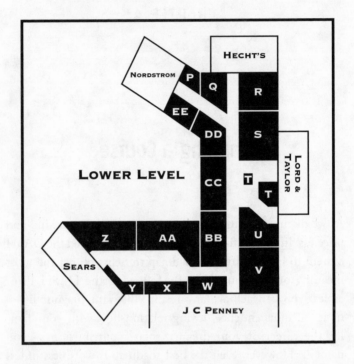

However, this map will be of limited use to you if you don't know where you are in the mall. For instance, let's suppose you are currently facing The Gap. From this map, it would appear that The Gap is one of the stores represented by a set of letters. The question is which letter? If The Gap is "X," then you simply need to head right for a short distance and you are there. On the other hand, what if The Gap is "CC"? In this case, heading right will take you to Hecht's, which is in the opposite direction of where you want to go.

Fortunately, the designers of these directories always include a large dot that says, "You are here." This dot allows you to easily navigate your way through the mall. Of course, you can only get so lost in a mall. Eventually, you will find your way to whatever store you want. The worst-case scenario is that you will waste 20 or 30 minutes.

However, finding your way through life is different. If you take a wrong turn in the mall of life, you can waste years or even decades of your life. Therefore, it is essential to ask yourself the question, "Where am I?"

Interestingly, this is a question that very few of us ever ask. In fact, in many cases, we avoid the answer to the question even when clues are available. For instance, when many people start experiencing credit difficulties, they stop opening the mail or answering the telephone. Instead of assessing their debts and making plans to deal with them, they attempt to "ignore" the debt out of existence. Of course, this strategy never works.

This is something I know firsthand. At various times in my life, I avoided asking the question "Where am I?" I let myself become blind to the problems that could have been solved easily. In fact, I became so blind to them that by the time my eyes were opened, it was too late. I was in a place that no one would ever want to be. I was in prison, locked away from everything and, most importantly, everyone that was important to me.

As you can see, I didn't write this book from the perspective of an academic or philosopher. The DASH Principles aren't esoteric ideas. They are real! The quality of my life has risen and fallen in direct relation to my adherence to them. When I've ignored these principles, I've suffered rejection, pain and isolation. And when I've embraced them, I've experienced joy, fulfillment and abundance.

Therefore, take a moment to note where you are in major areas of your life: career, finances, family relationships, health and spirituality. If you are like most people, the answer to the question "Where am I?" won't be straightforward. In some areas of your life, you will be in nirvana. And in other areas, you will be ... well, let's just say not nirvana. However, it's not so important where you are, but rather that you *know* where you are.

Remember, not everyone has the same goals in life. For instance, you may be perfectly satisfied with your financial situation even if you are doing just okay in that area. Not everyone feels the need to be Donald Trump. Likewise, if you are a young, single person, then family relationships may be less of a priority to you now than they will be five or ten years from now. Also, if you are retired or a stay-at-home parent, you may be past the point of caring about your current career status.

Also, please note that by including a spiritual component to this assessment, I'm not trying to push religion on you. Obviously, you are perfectly free to believe (or not believe) in whatever you like. In fact, The DASH System will work for you whether you are a Christian, Jew, Muslim, Buddhist – or none of the above. However, if you do have spiritual values, then it's important to keep them in mind. After all, as Jesus said, "What shall it profit a man if he shall gain the whole world, and lose his own soul in the process?"

WHERE DO YOU WANT TO GO?

Now that you know where you are, the next important question is where do you want to go? Your ability to answer this question will be the biggest factor in how meaningful your dash is to you. The simple truth is that all great accomplishments start with a goal.

Think for a moment about Neil Armstrong's walk on the moon. This remarkable achievement didn't happen by accident. Armstrong and his crew weren't just flying around aimlessly and decided that the moon looked like a good place to gas up, go to the restroom and grab a bite to eat. Instead, the moonwalk was the result of the painstaking effort of hundreds of people, and this effort began when John F. Kennedy set the *goal* of sending a man to the moon before the end of the 1960s.

The same is true for individual achievements. You must have a plan. In 1926, Gertrude Caroline Ederle became the first woman to swim the English Channel, taking 14 hours and 39 minutes to do it. I can't imagine that, when asked how she did it, she said, "Well, I just decided to go for a little swim and, before I knew it, I was in France."

THE POWER OF THE WRITTEN WORD

So let's get to work on setting some specific *written* goals for your dash. I've emphasized the word "written" because there is real power in writing down your goals. In fact, until a goal is written down, it's merely a wish.

In 1953, researchers conducted a study of the graduating class of Yale University. They interviewed the graduating seniors and discovered that only 3 percent of them had written goals for their lives. Thirty years later, researchers re-interviewed the graduates and discovered that the 3 percent with written goals were worth more in financial terms than the other 97 percent *combined*. There is real power in writing down your goals.

You've probably been introduced to this concept before. You may have even participated in a goal-setting workshop of some kind. You were probably asked to write down a list of everything you ever want to have, do, be or see in life. The good news is that I'm not going to ask you to do any of that. Now, please understand that making such a list works. For instance, if you write down every day that you want to go to England, then chances are excellent that you will go to England. However, the DASH System is about more than just helping you to acquire more stuff and visit more places. After all, if the only thing that your kids have to put on your tombstone is "Here Lies Mom. She Went to England," then your dash will have lacked some meaning.

> **"What we have done for ourselves alone dies with us; what we have done for others and the world remains and is immortal."**
> **—Albert Pike**

The purpose of this program is to help you make your dash as significant as possible. In other words, we're looking at the big picture. Having all the fame and fortune in the world won't necessarily add meaning to your life. I have acquired my fair share of both, but if that's all there is to say about me at the end of my dash, I've missed out on a major piece of the life puzzle.

Your Eulogy

Rather than making a list of your random impulses and desires, I suggest you write your eulogy. What are the things that you want people to say about you when you die? What kind of person were you? What kind of contribution did you make? What kind of legacy did you leave? It's crucial to ask these questions now, while you still have time to influence the answer.

I understand this task may seem somewhat morbid or self-obsessed, but the point is just the opposite. I want you to think about how your life affects others. At the end of your dash, no one but your heirs will care about your house, your money, your cars or your clothes. Instead, they will remember how you affected them. The purpose is to be clear on what you want that effect to be.

It's Time to Blast Off!

The countdown to New Year's Day is over. Have you blasted off yet?

For most people, this is the hardest part—just getting started. This is particularly true with New Year's resolutions. For many people, New Year's Day is a day for recuperation and relaxation as they spend the first day of their New Year nursing a hangover or watching the football games. And although there is surely nothing wrong with a little rest and relaxation, slacking off on the first day of the New Year makes it that much easier to slack off on the second day and the third and so on.

This is particularly true because the hardest part of starting on any new goal is just that—starting. In fact, getting off the launching pad takes more effort than the rest of the trip. For instance, when the space shuttle takes off, it expends more fuel in the first few miles of flight than it expends over the rest of its journey. As it tries to break the hold of gravity, it fires its thrusters at full blast. In fact, during its first few seconds of flight, it seems to be just inching forward. However, before long, the craft is hurtling through the sky at tremendous speeds. At this point, it releases two large fuel tanks, because from that point on, they are no longer necessary. The hard part of the trip is over.

Your journey through this year will be the same way. You will expend the greatest effort in breaking bad habits during the first few days of the year. For instance, if you resolved to quit smoking this year, the hardest day will be your first day without a cigarette. The same is true if you resolved to finally take off that extra 10, 25, or 100 pounds. Denying yourself that first slice of cheesecake will be harder than turning down the other hundred slices you will be offered this year. Likewise, stepping foot into the gym for the first time will be harder than all the other times *combined*.

This same principle applies to all goals. For instance, any salesperson will tell you that the hardest sale to make to a new client is the first sale. To make that first sale, a salesperson may have to call, visit, cajole, or downright beg the client for her business. However, the second sale is always much easier and the 100th sale seems to just happen automatically. Therefore, if you've set a goal to double or triple your sales this year (always a good goal to set), your most crucial month will be January. If you burn your thrusters at full strength during January, you will be cruising in September. However, if you choose to cruise through this month, you may find yourself grounded in mediocre results for another year.

Therefore, the day to get started on resolutions is TODAY. Now is the time to turn those New Year's *resolutions* into New Year's *realizations*. 3...2...1...Blast off!

THOUGHTS FOR YOUR DASH

Determination
"He has half the deed done who has made a beginning."
HORACE

Attitude
"Act like you expect to get into the end zone."
JOE PATERNO

Success
"The secret of getting ahead is getting started."
SALLY BERGER

Happiness
"The more you praise and celebrate your life, the more there is in life to celebrate."
OPRAH WINFREY

CHAPTER 5

The Devil is in the Details

After some thought, you should have a clear vision of what you want from your dash. This isn't to say that you should know *how* you are going to realize that vision. In fact, if you have a big dream, you may have no idea how you are going to make it happen. That's okay, because the purpose of this chapter is to help you create a map to get from where you are now to where you want to be in the future.

YOUR TRAVEL ITINERARY

Let me begin by saying that a map is <u>not</u> essential. You can make your dreams happen without first creating a plan. You could also drive from Seattle, Washington to Disney World without a map. However, in either case, the lack of a map will slow your progress and limit your options.

The Cross-Country Trip

For instance, you could easily drive to Disney World without a map by simply driving east. Eventually you would arrive at the Atlantic Ocean. Then you could simply turn the car south and continue down I-95 until you saw the signs for Disney World. It would work, but your journey wouldn't be optimal.

For one, this route would take you several hundred miles out of the way. By taking the time to first map out your route, you could save hours of driving time. Secondly, your journey won't be nearly as fun as it could have been had you taken the time to plan out your route. Between Seattle and Orlando, there are hundreds of amazing sights to see. However, if you travel without an itinerary, you will only be able to see those sights that happen to be along the highway you are traveling. This will be a tiny percentage of the sights available. Moreover, very few of these sights will be the ones that you would *choose* to see.

The "Cross-Life" Trip

As you can see, traveling without a map can be bad on a cross-country trip, but it's absolutely disastrous on a cross-*life* trip. First, the time wasted by not taking the most direct path can be years or decades. And time is the most valuable resource available to any of us. In fact, it's the only resource that is completely irreplaceable. For instance, if you lose $20,000 in the stock market, you can earn that money back through hard work. However, if you lose 20 years by taking an indirect route to your goal, there is nothing you can do to earn the time back. It is gone forever.

Second, as we'll discuss in detail later, happiness is not the destination – it's the journey. Your dash should bring you the greatest amount of satisfaction possible, so planning the journey is essential. By planning a cross-country trip beforehand, you can stop a few days at the Grand Canyon, see the Great Salt Lake, visit the Smithsonian, or see whatever it is that interests you. In fact, if you plan properly, you can have an incredible trip even if you never reach Orlando.

Your life should be the same way. You should be consistently moving toward a destination, but you also should be stopping along the way to "smell the roses." Even if you never reach your goal, you won't be bitter about your dash.

Your Special Destination

If you don't use a map, you will only be able to travel heavily visited places. For instance, let's suppose that instead of trying to get to Disney World, you were trying to visit your grandmother who lives in Orlando. Without specific directions, you could get to Orlando just fine. But in Orlando, there won't be any signs pointing the way to grandma's house. At this point, you are either going to have to get specific directions to grandma's house, get extremely lucky, or go to Disney World.

The same thing holds true for life. For instance, if you want to become wealthy, educated or lose 30 pounds, then you can follow the signposts. Your local bookstore is filled with books on each of these subjects. You could also find someone who is traveling your route and simply follow them to your destination.

The only problem with this approach is that your final destination is probably different from anyone else's. Remember, we are all unique and so are our goals and aspirations – or at least they should be. After all, no two of us even have the same fingerprints, so why should any two of us try to leave identical fingerprints on the world? Your mission should be unique to you, and this means that there won't be any pre-printed road signs or step-by-step instructional videos to guide the way.

Besides, what works for someone else may not work for you. For instance, there is a story of a woman who was driving home one night when a blanket of dense fog rolled into the area. Not able to see more than five feet in front of her, she began to closely follow the car in front of her. After several

55

miles, the car in front of her abruptly stopped and she ran into the back of it. She got out of her car, walked up to the other driver and angrily asked, "Why did you stop?" The other driver replied, "Because I'm in my garage."

This story is a metaphor for life. We often encounter situations in which the future looks foggy. At those times, it's tempting to allow someone else to navigate the unknown for us. However, we might end up going to *their* college or working in *their* job or marrying *their* ideal mate. Each of us must blaze our own trail.

Of course, we should look for assistance and guidance from time to time. In fact, in Chapters 15 and 16, I'll discuss in detail how to find coaches and mentors to provide "roadside assistance." However, in the final analysis, *you* are responsible for navigating your own course. Sure, you may have a few head-on collisions along the way, but at least you will be in control of your life.

CREATING YOUR PLAN

Let's talk about how to draft a travel plan. A good travel plan has two primary attributes: (1) it will get you where you want to go in a direct manner, and (2) it's feasible for *you*. We've already discussed the first part, so let's take a moment to discuss the second – feasibility.

Be Realistic

If your life plan is to be useful, it must take *you* into account – your talents, your proclivities and your situation. For instance, let's suppose you create a travel plan for your car trip to Disney World. In fact, you plan it out to the last detail – where you will eat, where you will sleep, where you will buy gas, etc. However, as detailed as your plan may be, it won't do you a bit of good if you don't have a car or a driver's license.

Not having a car shouldn't prevent you from going to Disney World. It simply means you will have to make alternate plans. For instance, you may have to fly, take a train or take a bus. If you really have your heart set on driving across the country, then you will have to first create a plan to get a car and a driver's license. The point is you can do anything you want in life, but some things will require an extra step (or two) of planning.

Be a Dreamer

I'm not suggesting that all your goals should be within your current abilities. In fact, I'm suggesting just the opposite. If you can easily achieve your goal, then you haven't set much of a goal at all. No one throws a party or holds a banquet for the person who accomplishes something that's easy to achieve. When was the last time someone congratulated you for having your shoes tied?

Sadly, setting low expectations is one of the primary causes for failure in life. The truth is that we will hit very few of our goals in life. This is why it's so important to aim high. If you shoot for the stars and even if you miss, you'll probably reach the moon. On the other hand, if you shoot for the moon and miss, then there is nothing left but to fall back to Earth.

> **"Keep your ideals high enough to inspire you and low enough to encourage you."**
> **—Unknown**

It took me six attempts at passing the broker's licensing exam before I learned this lesson for myself. The passing score on the exam is 70 out of 100. This is not a very difficult score to obtain. As a result, I didn't study the first five times I took the exam. Instead, I slept with the book under my pillow thinking that I could absorb enough through osmosis "to get by." The first five times I aimed for the minimum passing score and failed five times, I failed. Finally, I decided to take the test seriously and studied hard. In fact, I made it my goal to score 100 on the test. I missed this goal but, in the process, I finally passed the test.

In a sense, your goals should be like the stars. You may never succeed in reaching them, but like the great seafaring explorers of the past, you can use them to guide you to your ultimate destination. For instance, if one of your goals is to *always* be kind, then you are unlikely to ever reach this ideal. However, by guiding your life on the principle of kindness, you will live a life that is much more kind than most.

The Five Questions

For the sake of creating a game plan, let's assume you have a big aspiration – you want to reduce world hunger. In constructing your "travel itinerary" to make your dreams a reality, you will need to ask *and answer* the following five questions:

1. What do I love to do that can help fulfill my mission?

Could you use any of those activities to reach your mission? If so, then you now have a great chance for success because you have wedded your bliss and your purpose.

For instance, let's suppose one of your great loves is to write songs. If you had your choice, you would spend every Sunday morning at your piano. Could you find a way to use this activity to reduce world hunger? Of course, you could. Isn't that what a group of musicians in America did in the 1980s with the "We Are the World" song? They raised millions of dollars to feed starving children in third-world countries with a song.

Of course, if you're like most people, you will have a voice inside your head saying, "I'm not *that* good of a songwriter." Or worse, the voice will say, "I'm not rich and famous. Who's going to buy my song or play it on the radio?"

Ignore that voice for now. It raises some valid concerns that we will deal with later, but for now, the important thing is to understand that your best chance of reaching your goal is to let your bliss lead you to it.

For instance, if the problem is simply that you don't have the necessary skills to reach your goal, your bliss can handle it. If you love doing something, then you will take the effort necessary to improve at it. On the other hand, if you choose to pursue your mission by engaging in activities that you can barely tolerate, you will continually struggle towards your goal and most often you will fall short.

This happens often when people decide to lose weight. They decide to join a gym and "work out." And for the first two weeks or so, they do. They go to the gym three or four days a week and run on the treadmill, ride the stationary bicycles and lift weights. However, willpower only takes them so far. Eventually, the excuses start, "I have to work late," "I think I've pulled a muscle," "My dog ate my membership card," etc.

Has that ever happened to you? It's happened to most of us in one area or another. The way to avoid this problem is not by more discipline, but by wedding your bliss to your mission. Instead of working out, find a way to "play out." For instance, if you love dancing, then dance your way into shape. You won't find yourself making excuses to avoid doing what you love.

2. What kind of person must I be to achieve my purpose?

Someone once said, "We don't get in life what we want, we get what we are." For instance, if you are loving, generous and kind, then you usually get love, generosity and kindness in return. This happens even if you aren't consciously seeking those rewards. On the other hand, if you are petty, vindictive and cruel, then you usually get those things in return.

Take a look at your mission and decide what qualities you must possess to achieve it. Do you need to learn to be more organized, patient or courageous? If so, simply make a list of the qualities you will need in order to achieve your objective.

By the way, this isn't the time to start beating yourself up. After all, if you already had everything you needed to get what you want, then you'd already have it. Just think, at one point in life you couldn't walk, talk, read or write. However, as a baby, you didn't get depressed and throw in the towel. Instead, you simply went about acquiring those skills. The same process applies here.

3. Who are the people I will need to help me reach my objective?

You can't achieve a big goal by yourself. You are going to need the help of other people. And the bigger your objective, the more help you are going to need. After all, even the Lone Ranger had a buddy. Start making a list of the *type* of people and organizations whose help you'll need. And don't worry now if you don't know any of these people or can't think of a way to access them. With the tools that I will discuss in the "Attitude" and "Success" sections of this book, you will learn to attract these people into your life.

4. What resources will I need to achieve my goal?

With some of your goals, the answer to this question is going to be money, sometimes *lots* of money. In other cases, you will need resources like land, a boat, and so on. Regardless of what you need, the thing to do now is to simply list the necessary resources.

Once again, this isn't the time to panic. You will learn to attract everything you need to make your dream come true. However, you can only do so if you know what you need.

5. What can I do <u>today</u> to get started on this goal?

Yes, TODAY! The action may be to go to the library and pick up a few books on the subject of your goal. In fact, it could be as simple as making a phone call to one of the people on your list. Whatever it is, do it now!

The reason is simple. No plan, regardless of how brilliant or well-conceived, will work if you won't work. The critical ingredient of success is to get off your butt and do something. For instance, over the years, I've met several people who "invented" Federal Express. For years, these people *dreamed* about an overnight delivery service that would speed their business transactions. However, it took a man named Fred Smith to make this common dream come true. And he did it by taking *action*.

Regardless of how far away your goal may seem, there is something you can do today to bring it a little closer. Remember, "A journey of a thousand miles starts with a single step." So start stepping!

Be Flexible

You may notice that I've left out the usual advice about setting specific 5-, 10- and 20-year goals. This is because setting such long-range goals is unworkable in today's society. Change happens at such an incredibly fast pace in the 21st century that any plan made for five *years* from now will be worthless in five *months*.

The key to achieving long-range goals is to be flexible. Sure, the ultimate goal should be fixed and unmovable, but the building block goals are optional. For instance, when you get into your car to go to work, your ultimate destination is fixed. However, what if a particular road is closed for repairs? Do you just keep driving through the construction signs because that road is part of your plan or do you take a detour instead? Of course, the answer is that you take a detour.

During your dash, there will be many such detours and hurdles. Some of them can be predicted and plans put in place to deal with them when you hit them. However, there will be some unexpected hurdles that you must deal with on the spur of the moment. This is why it's so important to learn to be flexible.

> **"When you're through changing, you're through."**
> —Bruce Barton

Discipline is the Key

Have you ever locked your keys inside your car? If you have, then you know what a frustrating experience this can be. You stand helplessly outside of *your* car—the car that you pay for, put gas into, and take for oil changes and tune-ups. Yet none of those things matter to your car door's locking mechanism. It simply responds to the key. If you have it, you can get in. If you don't, then you can't. The locks on the doors to the real treasures of life (wealth, health, love, friendship, spirituality, and peace of mind) are the same way. These "locks" will only respond to one thing—the key—and that key is discipline.

With discipline, you have full access to the treasure chamber. Without discipline, you will be locked out of the wealth of opportunities available to you. And no amount of pleading, banging, screaming, or cursing will help you. Success is deaf to everything but the turning of the key of discipline. In fact, after a lifetime of studying the wealthiest men and women in America, Napoleon Hill, the author of *Think and Grow Rich*, concluded, "Self-discipline is the master key to riches."

Of course, "riches" mean more than just money. Discipline can help you acquire any form of abundance, even health. For example, let's suppose you decide to improve your health by eating better, exercising regularly, and quitting smoking. You go to the library and check out several books on good nutrition, exercise programs, and smoking cessation. You then take the next step by shopping at a health food store, joining a gym, and throwing out all of your cigarettes, ashtrays, and lighters. At this point, are you any healthier? Of course not.

Although these are useful first steps, your health will not change for the better until you exercise the *discipline* to eat the healthy foods you bought, work out consistently at the gym you joined, and steer clear of smoking. All these actions require just one attribute on your part—discipline. If you discipline yourself to do these things, you *will* improve your health. The results are guaranteed. They don't depend upon the economy, support from your in-laws, and the weather. Your success is guaranteed so long as you have discipline.

When I finally learned this truth, my life began to take off. Up until that point, I thought that you had to be smart, attractive, or popular to be successful. Because I didn't think of myself as any of these things, I thought I was doomed to a life of mediocrity. However, when I learned that the ultimate key to success was discipline, I got excited. You don't have to have an IQ of 180 to be disciplined. You don't have to have a degree from Harvard to be disciplined. You don't have to have had a perfect childhood to be disciplined. Every one of us can acquire discipline. And like most things in life, it's not nearly as difficult as you would imagine.

In fact, acquiring discipline is quite simple. It merely requires making a commitment and then keeping it. This is something we all do every day. We make commitments to our customers, our employers, our creditors, our spouses, our children, our church, etc.... In most cases, we keep these commitments. However, discipline requires one more thing; that we keep the commitments we make to ourselves, whether that commitment is to lose weight, quit smoking, save money, give to charity, or complete a degree.

For some reason, this seems to be tricky for most people, so let me give you just a few tools to help you improve your discipline:

Make a Commitment—A commitment is more than a wish. A commitment means that you *will* achieve a certain result. This is not the same thing as wishing or hoping to achieve it. With a true commitment, there are no excuses. You must decide that nothing will prevent you from reaching your personal objective and then you must act accordingly.

Pay Yourself Often—We often set goals and say to ourselves, "When I finally accomplish A, B, and C, I will get this great reward." The problem with this approach is that the reward is too far off in the future. It's difficult to keep your end of the bargain if the payoff is remote. When you get the urge to back out on your commitment (and you will), you need a more immediate reward. Think about it. Would you work for your current employer if you were only paid once every five years? Sure, that would be one HUGE paycheck, but could you keep your nose to the grindstone for five years waiting for it? So, just as you are paid every week, two weeks, or month by your employer, pay yourself a regular "salary" for keeping your commitment. Give yourself a gift of a shopping spree, a night out on the town, a weekend at a spa, or just a long, hot bath for keeping your commitment.

Make It Hurt—One of the reasons we are so good in keeping commitments to others is because we know they won't let us off the hook. For instance, if you renege on your commitment to pay your mortgage, your lender won't call and say, "Oh, that's alright. I know there was a big sale at the mall last week. Just make it up when you can." However, that's exactly what you might say to yourself if you fail to meet a commitment to save money, clean out the garage, or spend more time at church. To make sure you keep your commitments to yourself, you need to establish consequences. After all, if you don't make your car payment, you will have to take the bus. So why not apply the same principle with your most important creditor—you? Establish negative consequences for failing to meet your commitments and then stick to them. Trust me; it won't take more than one or two Saturday nights of being "grounded" to make you take your commitments seriously.

Try Again—I don't care how disciplined you are, you will let yourself down from time to time. When this happens, take your punishment like a man (or a woman), recommit, and try again. Discipline is like any other skill; it takes practice. You didn't learn to walk on your first try or swim on your first day in the pool, so cut yourself some slack, and realize that this is a process. Remember, you will never become *completely* disciplined. The goal is to become *more* disciplined, so keep at it.

"Don't get discouraged; it's usually the last key in the bunch that opens the lock."

Author Unknown

THOUGHTS FOR YOUR DASH

Determination
> "Losers make promises they often break. Winners make commitments they always keep."
>> DENIS WAITLEY

Attitude
> "Live your beliefs and you can turn the world around."
>> HENRY DAVID THOREAU

Success
> "The elevator to success is out of order. You'll have to use the stairs...one step at a time."
>> JOE GIRARD

Happiness
> "I believe God is managing affairs and that He doesn't need any advice from me. With God in charge, I believe everything will work out for the best in the end. So what is there to worry about?"
>> HENRY FORD

Part Two

ATTITUDE

"Attitude is a controlled force that will navigate
the results of your life."
—Eric J. Aronson

CHAPTER 6

It's as Easy as One, Two, Three

Who are you? As basic as this question may seem, most of us have never had to answer it. When we are introduced to people at social functions, they never ask "Who are you?" Instead, they usually ask, "What do you *do* for a living?" In other settings, people may ask what we own – "Do you own a house?" or "What kind of car do you drive?"

Over time, we become skilled at answering these questions. In fact, we even learn to create fancy titles and pithy sayings, "Well, George, I'm a real estate sales professional. I sell dreams." Likewise, we all know the year, make and model of our cars; the balances in our savings and investment accounts; and the equity in our homes. And don't get me wrong, there is nothing wrong with being able to answer the questions about what you do or what you have.

However, you must keep in mind that you are not a human *doing* nor are you a human *having*. You are a human *being*. Therefore, the chief question to answer in life is "Who do you *be*?" Now, I understand that this is a terrible question from a grammatical point of view, but from a DASH point of view, it is the key question. What

71

kind of person are you? What kind of person do you aspire to be?

THE THREE STEPS OF ACHIEVEMENT

The simple truth is that success in life is a three-step process: being, doing and having. And the process must be followed in that order. In other words, in order to have, you must first do. But before you can do, you must be. I know this probably sounds backwards, but let me explain.

For instance, let's suppose you desire wealth. You are probably thinking that once you have wealth, you will *be* wealthy but in truth, it's the other way around. Once you become wealthy, you will then be able to do the things that will give you the wealth. Still not convinced? I didn't think so.

The Long-Term View

Let me use an example to make my point. For instance, let's suppose your average Joe (let's call him "Fred") wins $2 million in the lottery. However, I still contend that Fred is not wealthy. Fred simply happens to have a lot of money in the bank. You may ask, "What's the difference?" Well, there's a big difference.

For instance, if someone feels well on a particular day, would you say that they are necessarily a "healthy" person? Of course not. Just the same way that if someone feels ill on a particular day, you wouldn't conclude that they were "unhealthy." The level of someone's health is not measured over the course of a single day but over the course of a lifetime. And the level of someone's wealth is measured the same way.

Therefore, if Fred is like most lottery winners, he will be flat broke within three years. Fred's three years of money in the bank will not have made him wealthy, any more than three years of good health makes a person healthy.

On the other hand, let's take a look at someone like

Donald Trump. Trump has had some remarkable reversals of fortune over the years. During the 1980s, he became internationally known as one of America's richest men. Then, during the 1990s, he saw his net worth virtually evaporate. Now, he is once again on top. However, there has been no time in the last 20 years when Donald Trump was "poor." Sure, there were times when his balance sheet didn't look too healthy, but that was simply a short-term situation. After all, even the healthiest person in the world gets sick every once in a while.

The DASH System is devoted to your **long-term** success and happiness. I'm not interested in helping you have one good month or one good year or one good decade. I want you to have a good *life*. That's why this system has been built on principles, one of which is the "be-do-have" process. Once you become the kind of person you want to **be**, you will automatically **do** the things required for you to **have** what you want out of your dash.

There Are No Shortcuts

If your goal is to become wealthy, the first step is for you to start thinking like a wealthy person. You must develop the mindset of a rich person. Of course, having the right mindset alone will not add any more zeros to your net worth. The next step will be for you to start acting like a wealthy person – attracting and capitalizing on wealth-creating opportunities. Only then will you have the wealth that you desire.

You may be thinking, "Why do I need the first step? If I just do what wealthy people do, won't I become wealthy too?" The answer is yes. However, you need to develop the wealth mindset before you can take action. After all, don't you know at least one way to get rich? Of course you do!

We all understand the concept of compound interest and

that a relatively small amount of money can grow into a huge sum over time. For instance, just $100 per month invested at 12 percent would yield more than $1 million in 40 years. As you can see, almost anyone can become a millionaire by retirement. It simply requires taking $100 from your first paycheck and doing that every month until retirement. However, how many Americans follow this plan?

The sad truth is very few of us. Why? After all, if it's this simple to be a millionaire, why don't we all do it? I suspect that it's for the same reasons that all of us don't eat healthily, exercise regularly and quit destructive habits like drinking and smoking. Knowledge is not enough.

We all *know* several actions we could take to make our lives better. The real problem is by taking these actions, we only take consistent action when we "become" the change we wish to see. At that point, we become compelled to take the actions necessary to make our circumstances fit into our self-image of ourselves.

From a financial standpoint, I call this the "broke, busted and disgusted" theory of transformation. For the first few years of my adult life, I struggled financially, living from paycheck to paycheck. At the end of each month, I had nothing to show for my efforts. I was broke. However, it wasn't all bad. I had money for movies, dates and nights out with the guys. In fact, I probably could have continued along that way for a while. After all, many Americans live paycheck to paycheck. However, in addition to being broke, I always seemed to be "busted." A major appliance would need repair or my car would break down. As a result, not only was I not making any financial headway but I was also going deeper into the hole.

However, even being broke and busted was not enough for me to change my financial situation. My financial situation didn't truly change until I also became "disgusted." One day, I finally said, "I've had it! I'm no longer willing to live like this!" However, that day only arrived *after* my self-image had improved to the point where it was no longer acceptable for the new "rich" me to live like a pauper. It was only at that point that I started taking the actions necessary to make sure that I lived the kind of lifestyle that I wanted.

Hitting Rock Bottom

From my experience, this is what happens to everyone who makes a drastic change. For instance, people who overcome drug addiction only do so after hitting "rock bottom." This is the point where they realize they deserve a better life than the one they're living.

Interestingly, rock bottom is not the same for everyone. For some people, rock bottom occurs when they are arrested or jailed. For others, rock bottom only occurs when they've lost everything they own. And for others, rock bottom doesn't occur until they overdose or become seriously ill. So what's the difference? It comes down to self-image. Regardless of whether the problem is drugs, obesity, smoking, debt or marital strife, nothing much changes until your mind says, "I deserve better than this!"

This is why it's so important to change your self-image or attitude about yourself. As long as your current mindset says, "This is all I deserve," then *this* is all you get. On the other hand, once you become convinced that you deserve better, you will make the necessary changes.

Take the Easy Way Out

Recently, I called a friend to compliment him on yet another successful project. In turn, he complimented me on a recent deal that I'd put together. Before long, our conversation resembled a meeting of the Mutual Admiration Society. I'd compliment him and he'd say, "That's nothing. What's amazing is how you did...." And I'd reply, "Oh please! That's simple. What's hard is the way you did...."

If someone had been eavesdropping on our conversation, he or she would probably have thought that we were being falsely modest. Yet, the truth is that neither of us is tremendously impressed with our own accomplishments. This is because they come easily to us. In short, we take the easy way out.

By taking the easy way out, I don't mean that we take shortcuts or give less than our best efforts. What I do mean is that we concentrate our efforts on those things that come easiest to us. For example, sales and marketing comes easily to me. On the other hand, organization and record keeping isn't my strong suit. As a result, I spend most of my time engaged in sales and marketing and almost none of my time organizing files or keeping records. The same is true for my friend, who is a gifted communicator and spends most of his time doing just that.

In fact, taking the easy way out is the key to success for most super successful people. For instance, do you think Bill Gates started programming computers as a teenager because he knew that it would be a multibillion-dollar industry? Perhaps, but I doubt it. I suspect that he started programming computers for the same reason that

Michael Jordan started shooting hoops and Barry Bonds started hitting baseballs—it came easily to him.

What comes easily to you? Are you really good with your hands? Or are you a really creative person who can create colorful stories and characters? Or are you a natural at planning and organization? Or are you naturally gifted with people? Can you walk into a room and instantly strike up a conversation with anyone? Whatever it is that comes easily to you, that's what you should be spending your time doing.

By taking the easy way out, you greatly increase your chances for success. Sure, you can't just coast on natural ability. You need to hone your craft. However, by working on a craft in which you have a natural ability, you greatly improve your chances of achieving mastery.

On the other hand, by trying to do something for which you don't have a natural inclination, you almost certainly guarantee failure. For one thing, the level of frustration at the early stages will tempt you to throw up your hands and ask, "What's the use?" And even if you are tough enough not to quit, you will most likely scale back your expectations. You'll correctly perceive that if it was hard for you at the beginning level, then you have almost no chance at the advanced levels. Therefore, at best, you will consign yourself to a life of mediocrity, in which your aim is to just "get by."

For me, just getting by in a world full of opportunities to "get ahead" is unacceptable. And as someone who is taking the time to read this newsletter, you probably feel the same way. You want (and deserve) to enjoy the best that life has to offer and, ironically, the way to make the most out of your DASH is to "take the easy way out."

"The road to happiness lies in two simple principles: find what it is that interests you and that you can do well, and when you find it put your whole soul into it—every bit of energy and ambition and natural ability you have."

John D. Rockefeller

THOUGHTS FOR YOUR DASH

Determination
> "A man of ability and the desire to accomplish something can do anything."

Donald Kircher

Attitude
> "When we accept tough jobs as a challenge to our ability and wade into them with joy and enthusiasm, miracles can happen."

Arland Gilbert

Success
> "It is not enough to be good if you have the ability to be better."

Alberta Lee Cox

Happiness
> "Basing our happiness on our ability to control everything is futile."

Stephen Covey

CHAPTER 7

"I Think I Can, I Think I Can"

The first step to achieving your mission in life, regardless of the mission, is to believe that you are worthy. Noted author and business consultant Dr. Michael LeBoeuf says, "The greatest single determinant of what you will be or do with your creative abilities is your perception of who you are. Self-esteem is central to the whole problem of securing any type of success in any endeavor."

A healthy sense of who you are is essential to making your dash all that it can be. This is why I spend so much time stressing your value, worth and uniqueness. However, it really doesn't matter what *I* think about you. Nor does it matter what your parents, friends or colleagues think about you. In the end, what matters is what *you* think about you.

ARONSON'S THEORY OF RELATIVITY

$$E=MC^2$$

Excellence = Motivation x Confidence^2

SELF-CONFIDENCE

Self-confidence is the attitude that allows you to have a positive, yet realistic, view of yourself and your situation. You trust your own abilities, have a general sense of control in your life and believe that, within reason, you will be able to do what you wish, plan and expect. You are willing to risk the disapproval of others because you genuinely trust your own abilities. You tend to accept yourself and don't feel you have to conform to be accepted.

How is your self-confidence? This is an important area of your life to take an honest assessment. For some people, self-confidence comes easily. However, for most of us (myself included), self-confidence is a difficult thing to develop. Moreover, even a generally self-confident person will lack self-confidence in some area of life. For instance, you may feel completely comfortable with your ability to handle the challenges of work but not the challenges of your family life. Or you may feel like a lion in the area of spirituality, but a lamb when it comes to personal finances.

The good news is that anyone can develop self-confidence. It simply takes some training and practice but who would deny that it's worth it? The important thing is to notice any area where your lack of confidence is stopping you from doing what you know you should and then attack that area. For instance, if you lack confidence in the area of personal finance and you've been procrastinating about starting a savings plan, this is an area you need to address.

The goal is not to become a champion in every area, but rather to be confident enough to know you can handle challenges you may face in those areas.

Cut Yourself Some Slack

The key to developing self-confidence is to cut yourself some slack. Don't feel you must do everything perfectly or you're a failure. For instance, you need not be the "perfect parent" or "perfect spouse" or "perfect employee" in order to feel good about yourself in any of those roles. Instead of looking for perfection, look for improvement. In that way, you judge yourself not based on some unreachable ideal, but on how far you've come. The goal is to be as good as you can be. The expression that I try to live up to is:

> *I ain't what I want to be,*
> *I ain't what I'm gonna to be,*
> *But thank God I ain't what I was.*

Try Something New

By eliminating perfection as your goal, you allow yourself to take risks and try new things. Think about it. When was the last time that you tried to do something new – a new sport, a new dance or a new hobby? If you are like most people, it may have been *years* since you tried something new. As adults, we get this crazy idea in our heads that we must be good at everything we do. And since we are not usually good at things that are new to us, we don't even try them.

But this is ridiculous. How are you ever supposed to become good at anything without first going through the learning process? Remember, you were once terrible at *everything*, even things you now do very well. If you are now an excellent salesperson, think back to your first sales call. Were you a smooth operator? I doubt it. You probably stuttered and stammered your way through that first presentation. Likewise, if you are now an excellent cook, think back to the first meal you prepared. Was it even edible? In any event, I'm sure that it wasn't "perfect."

Emerson once said, "Unless you try to do something beyond what you have already mastered, you will never grow."

You simply cannot grow if you take yourself too seriously. If you are obsessed with always being perfect, you will miss out on the new and exciting opportunities that are available to you.

The next time you're at a party, jump onto the dance floor and start doing the latest line dance. Likewise, if you have a chance to sing at karaoke bar, take it. You might be saying, "But I have two left feet" or "I couldn't carry a tune with a bucket." That's OK. The point is not to be discovered by talent scouts from Star Search, but to lose the sense of embarrassment that comes from not being perfect.

As long as the fear of embarrassment holds any power in your life, you will never be free to be all that you can be. You constantly will be held back for fear that other people will laugh at you or think less of you. However, when you think about it, every person who has ever done anything great has been the subject of ridicule – or worse. Can you imagine what people must have said to Christopher Columbus when he told them that he was going to sail to the New World? Or can you imagine the weird looks the Wright Brothers must have received as they ran back and forth across a hill at Kitty Hawk, trying to get their flying machine airborne?

Great men and women didn't let the fear of being ridiculed stop them from changing the course of history. They understood that the only way to avoid criticism is to do nothing, say nothing and be nothing. But where's the fun in that? Besides, the only opinion of you that really matters is your own.

Ignore Negative Programming

Unfortunately, we often adopt our self-image from others, and sometimes that image is undeservedly negative. Think about Cinderella. She was criticized daily by her stepmother and stepsisters. When she told them of her dream of going to the ball, they laughed and belittled her. According to them, she was too ugly and uncultured to even dare consider going to the ball.

In fact, when her fairy godmother first suggested that she go to the ball, Cinderella herself opposed the idea. Parroting the words she had heard most of her life, she repeated that she was too ugly, too poor and too uncultured to be in the presence of a prince. Even after the fairy godmother provided her with a beautiful gown and a horse-drawn carriage, Cinderella was reluctant to go to the ball. But she finally relented, and we all know the rest of the story.

Although Cinderella is just a fairytale, many of us suffer from the Cinderella Syndrome in real life. I was one such person. As a child, I was diagnosed as ADD, ADHD, ODD, etc. Of course, back then we didn't have fancy names and acronyms, so I was just labeled as being plain old B-A-D. Over time, even I became convinced that my natural eagerness, curiosity and initiative were bad things. As a result, I lived down to the level of these expectations all through school. I acted like a "bad kid," and my grades and behavior reflected my actions.

Leaving high school as Mr. Most Likely Not To Succeed, I bounced around from job to job, never really applying myself. After all, who was I to make something of myself? I was one of the "bad kids." My life only changed by happenstance when I met my "fairy godfather."

This man encouraged me to become a stockbroker. At first I resisted his encouragement because I simply didn't see myself as "that type of person." At the time, I didn't know what "that type of person" was, but I knew that it wasn't me. Over time, my fairy godfather showed me a vision of myself that made me see that I was "that kind of person."

Adopt a Fairy Godparent

If you were unfortunate enough to have similar experiences, then let me be your fairy godfather. Let me tell you that you are not too ugly, too poor or too uncultured to go to the ball. You have all the brains, beauty, talent and courage you'll ever need to make your dash whatever you want it to be.

However, as your fairy godfather, please note that I will be working with two restrictions. For one, I can only use what you already have to help you make the transformation. Just as in the fairy tale, Cinderella's fairy godmother didn't create a new gown for her but rather transformed her old rags. Therefore, over the course of this book, please note that all of your newfound and shiny success will simply be a transformation of the "rags" you've been wearing all along.

Secondly, any "magic" I can work will only be temporary. In *Cinderella*, the fairy godmother's magic worked only until the stroke of midnight. After that, Cinderella was on her own to learn that she was worthy of the handsome prince's love. Hopefully, this book will work the same magic for you. My sincere hope is that you will read something that gives you a vision of just how wonderful your dash can be. However, that vision won't last forever. It will be up to you to carry that vision forward in your own mind and to make it a reality. If you are willing to work together under those two restrictions, then let's get to work!

Keep the Pressure On

In teaching the DASH Principles to people across the country, I make a lot of promises. I promise that by faithfully living by these principles, people can achieve greater wealth, health, and happiness. I promise that the DASH Principles will help people to achieve more fulfilling family relationships and a sense of purpose. However, I never promise that the DASH Principles will relieve the pressures of life. In fact, just the opposite is true. As you constantly strive to make the most out of your DASH, you can be assured that you will encounter more than your fair share of pressures.

However, this is a good thing. Pressure is a key driving force in life. And although we normally associate pressure with anxiety, stress, and overwhelming hardship, the truth of the matter is that pressure also adds excitement, exhilaration, and joy to our lives. Of course, as with all things in life, you must achieve a balance. Yet, if you're going to err on one side or the other, I would suggest that you err on the side of pressure. After all, as bad as high blood pressure is for you, it's a lot better for you than *no* blood pressure.

Right now, blood is pumping through your entire body through the use of pressure. Without this pressure, gravity would pull all the blood into your feet, leaving no blood (or oxygen) in your upper extremities, including your brain. And although there are some members of Congress who seem to be able to get along just fine in this condition, you and I would be in serious trouble in this state. We need this internal pressure to survive.

Well, if you're going to *thrive* in your life, you'll need external pressure. You can only reach your maximum potential when you're being "pushed" by some external pressure. If you're an athlete, then you're probably at your best when you face your stiffest competition. The same is true in business. You reach your peak in terms of resourcefulness and efficiency when a coworker is after your job or a competitor is after your clients. However, without pressure, we all tend to become victims of gravity and slowly drift downward in terms of our performance.

In my view, the key to getting the most out of your life is to control the pressure in your life as opposed to being controlled by the pressure. The question is not whether you will have pressure in your life. The question is what type of pressure it will be. Will it be a self-imposed pressure or a pressure dictated by circumstances? Self-imposed pressures allow you to take better control of your life.

For instance, you can take control of your health by putting pressure on yourself to lose weight or quit smoking or you can deal with the pressure of suffering from a heart attack or stroke down the road. Likewise, you can put pressure on yourself to spend more time with your spouse or you can deal with the pressure of a divorce. In the end, the choice is yours.

One way to establish pressure on ourselves is to set some firm deadlines. Often, people *intend* to reduce their debt, start a business, or take a vacation to Greece. However, they never set a firm deadline for doing so. They simply assign these tasks to the magical day of "someday." The problem is that someday is never *today*. As a result, they find themselves never really making any progress toward these objectives. The way to solve this problem is to establish *firm* deadlines for their completion.

By a firm deadline, I mean a deadline for which there are rewards for meeting the deadline or consequences for missing it. A classic example of a firm deadline is April 15. The vast majority of Americans file their tax returns (or obtain an extension) by this deadline. Why? Because there are severe consequences for not doing so. What do you think would happen if this deadline were not so firm? Do you think people would stand in line at the post office at 11:59 p.m. on April 15 to meet a "suggested" deadline? Probably not. In fact, some Americans would never "get around" to filing a return at all.

Without a firm deadline, you may never get around to taking the action required to fulfill your destiny. Therefore, make sure that you set (and keep) your own firm deadlines in life. By keeping the pressure on yourself, you can prevent a lot of unwanted pressure from the outside world. As Zig Ziglar says, "If you have enough push, you don't have to worry about the pull."

"Under the pressure of trial and responsibility we are often stronger than when there is no pressure."

Mark Rutherford

Determination
> "Give me a stock clerk with a goal and I'll give you a man who will make history. Give me a man with no goals and I'll give you a stock clerk."
>
> J. C. PENNEY

Attitude
> "Too many people overvalue what they are not and undervalue what they are."
>
> MALCOLM S. FORBES

Success
> "If I had only done today what I set out for yesterday I'd be free tomorrow."
>
> ANDY MUNTHE

Happiness
> "The reason why worry kills more people than work is that more people worry than work."
>
> ROBERT FROST

CHAPTER 8

Thoughts are Things

In my travels, I encounter people of all different nationalities, races, cultures and religions. And although all of these people are unique individuals, I can honestly say that they can be put into just two groups – the people who think they can and the people who think they can't. And the truly amazing thing about both groups is that they are absolutely correct.

The person who thinks she can finish college invariably earns a college degree, sometimes several degrees. The person who thinks he's too stupid or too lazy to earn a college degree doesn't finish. In fact, most often, this person won't even take the time to enroll in school in the first place. What's the use? Richard M. Devos, co-founder of Amway, put it like this:

"The only thing that stands between a man and what he wants from life is often merely the will to try it and the faith to believe that it is possible."

GIGO AND TITO

As children, we all heard the expression "you are what

you eat," and there is some truth to that old adage. If you feed your body cookies, ice cream and cake, your body will become soft, lumpy and gelatinous. However, you are not only a body, but also a brain. And by now, you know that your brain is a hundred times more valuable than your body. Therefore, it's equally important to watch what you feed your mind.

In computer terminology, the term is GIGO – garbage in, garbage out. In short, the validity of your output will depend primarily on the validity of your input. For instance, let's suppose we were using a computer to calculate the area of a rectangle. The formula for this calculation is:

$$Area = Length \times Width$$

This is a very simple calculation. In fact, if the numbers are small enough, then a computer is not even necessary. We could easily arrive at the right answer using a calculator or by just doing the math in our heads. All that's required is that we input the correct values for length and width. On the other hand, if our input is incorrect, then even a NASA supercomputer won't get us to the right answer.

Well, the same principle applies to the most phenomenal supercomputer the world has ever known – your mind. If you input data into your brain that you are not a good leader, your brain will produce results based on that data. Likewise, if you input data into your brain that you are not smart enough, talented enough or strong enough, your brain will work to give you a result based on that data. This is the case whether this data is true or false.

Fortunately, the process also works the other way around. Besides operating on the principle of GIGO, our brains also operate on the principle of TITO – treasure in, treasure out. If you dump data in your brain about your strengths, your brain will dump out corresponding results. Your expectations often control your results.

WHAT IS REAL?

The bottom line is that thoughts are things. This may sound like a radical statement but philosophers have been speaking of this truth for centuries. More than 2,000 years ago, Buddha said, "We are what we think." Virgil said, "They can because they think they can." Each of these historical giants understood that our thoughts control our circumstances, and even our happiness. And each of these men lived in times of limited understanding.

In the 20th century, scientists have discovered some fundamental truths about the universe that provide further support for the theory that thoughts are things. With the discovery of quantum physics, we learned that matter consists of waves of energy. The objects we previously thought of as "solid" are actually nothing more than waves of energy carrying particles.

Our understanding of these waves in the last century changed our lives in ways that would have been unimaginable to our great grandparents. We now use microwaves to beam television images across the globe seemingly simultaneously. We use radio waves to beam signals into our homes, our cars and even to handheld radios that we can listen to while out jogging. Could you even imagine going to a hospital today that didn't have the ability to take x-rays or ultrasounds?

And I have not even mentioned the most amazing type of wave – the thought wave. Just as particles ride on the waves of other types of energy, particles also ride on thought waves. However, don't take my word for it. David Bohm, a famous quantum physicist, had this to say:

"Since matter is waves of energy and thought is energy, matter and thought are different aspects of the same thing. Thus, our thoughts and what we manifest and create from them are merely the constructs of our minds. The systems and institutions under which we live, and the scales by which we measure, come from the way we think. Our questions determine our answers."

Besides, even without any quantum physics theories, we have all experienced thoughts as things. How many times have you "felt" someone staring at you? Or how many times have you been thinking of someone just to have them call you or show up on your doorstep at that very moment? These things happen to us all the time.

Now, please don't misunderstand me. I'm not suggesting you start a psychic hotline. I'm simply suggesting that since your thoughts are things, you must appreciate that they have *real* power. In fact, everything we create in the physical world originates from our minds, or more specifically, the way we think.

"Change your thoughts, and you change your world."
—Norman Vincent Peale

THOUGHTS MOVE THE WORLD

On one level, this is fairly obvious. Obviously, the automobile, airplane and even the Swiss army knife were created by people using their brains. However, the implications of this truth are profound because it means that we are in the driver's seat in life. Our reality isn't controlled by our parents, our bosses, the economy or "the breaks," but rather by our thoughts. By controlling our thoughts, we can create what we want in our lives.

This is a powerful concept that is at the heart of the

DASH System, and it's derived from rock-solid scientific evidence. In the same way that you can trust the principles of microwave technology and radio technology to fly in an airplane, you can trust this principle to make your dash *anything* you want it to be.

Therefore, it's crucial for us to control our thoughts, as they determine what we experience in life. If we think about joy and abundance, then we generally experience joy and abundance. On the other hand, if we think about misery and pain, we experience those things too.

> **"The mind is its own place, and in itself can make heaven of hell, a hell of heaven."**
> **—John Milton**

It's Time for Spring-Cleaning

Once again, it's time for a little spring-cleaning. It's time to wash the windows, clear the gutters, and clean out the attic. And while you're at it, you may want to take a few minutes to do some mental spring-cleaning as well.

Winter isn't just a season on the calendar; it's also a season of life. We experience a winter whenever we have a period when things don't go well. We experience winters in business when sales fall and our productivity decreases. We experience winters in our relationships when the passion fades and arguments ensue over even the smallest things. We experience winters in our health when we get hurt or sick. During the course of your DASH, you'll experience many winters, but the good news is that they will all eventually turn into spring.

And when spring finally rolls around, it's important to clean up after winter's effects. For instance, in a geological winter, your house is pelted with rain, sleet, and snow so that by the time spring rolls around, your windows are covered in crud. It becomes difficult to even see out of them. Well, the same is true when you've been through a personal winter. You've been pelted with rejection, hostility, loneliness, pain, etc. By the end of your winter, it's difficult to see all the beautiful and positive things in your life. That's why you must wipe your mental windows clean.

But how do you do this? Amazingly, the process is remarkably similar to washing dirt off your windows or any other surface for that matter. The key thing you're trying to accomplish is to detach the dirt from the object. If the dirt has been recently applied, then you simply need to wipe it off. However, if the dirt has become caked onto the object, you may need to scrub, spray, or peel it off. The same thing applies to cleaning the dirt that becomes caked into your mind. You may have to put a little "elbow grease" into your efforts by reading a good self-help book, watching an inspiring movie, hearing a stirring sermon, or using positive affirmations. The important thing is to keep scrubbing until you can clearly see all the beauty in your DASH.

Another thing you must clean out around your house is the clogged storm drains or gutters. It's amazing how much stuff can become clogged up in there. Before long, the drain is completely blocked. Well, the storm drains of your mind can become just as blocked up. During your personal winter, the leaves of discontent may have been blown into your mental drains so often that you've become stuck. As a result, you no longer believe that you have the ability to maintain a healthy relationship, effectively parent your children, responsibly handle money, or what have you.

Obviously, none of these things is true. However, they'll be your reality so long as you believe them. Remember, as Henry Ford once said, "Whether *you* think you can or you think you can't, you're right." Therefore, you must get rid of this mental refuse, and there are two ways to do it. One way is to reach inside ourselves and pull out the hurt, rejection, and feelings of failure a little bit at a time until our drains are clear again. The only problem with that method is that sometimes the tube is too narrow or too long to reach all the way inside. Therefore, the better way may be to clear your mental gutters with a blower. You simply blow in enough thoughts of love, power, strength, and courage that the mental garbage is thrown out the other side.

Another big part of spring-cleaning is cleaning out the attic or the garage. It's simply amazing how much junk we can accumulate between Thanksgiving and Easter. Well, the same is true during your personal winter. You can accumulate bad habits, troublesome friends, time-wasting hobbies, etc. All these things clutter up your life and take time and space away from the things that can help you to make the most of your DASH. For this reason, an essential part of mental spring-cleaning is throwing away some of these old habits, activities, and relationships.

Of course, I understand that this is a difficult thing to do. After all, it's hard enough to throw away clothes; sometimes just for fear that they might come back in style. It's even harder to throw away old habits and familiar past times. And it's especially difficult to give up personal relationships, even when they are toxic or negative. Yet, all these things are necessary to make room for new habits, new hobbies, and new relationships.

As your personal winter breaks and the sun begins to shine on your life again, take a few hours to do some mental spring-cleaning. The spring, summer, and fall of your DASH have many blessings to offer but these blessings can't reach you behind cloudy windows, clogged drains, and cluttered entryways.

"If we had no winter, the spring would not be so pleasant: if we did not sometimes taste of adversity, prosperity would not be so welcome."

Anne Bradstreet

THOUGHTS FOR YOUR DASH

Determination
    "A thick skin is a gift from God."
Konrad Adenauer

Attitude
    "Life is 10 percent what you make it and 90 percent how you take it."
Irving Berlin

Success
    "If you don't quit, and don't cheat, and don't run home when trouble arrives, you can only win."
Shelley Long

Happiness
    "No winter lasts forever; no spring skips its turn."
Hal Borland

CHAPTER 9

The Thought Police

Now that you understand using the true power of your thoughts to shape your reality, you may be asking, "How do I control my thoughts?" After all, it seems like thoughts just pop into our heads at the most random times. For instance, you may be working on a project and, all of a sudden, you remember a joke you heard over the weekend.

The key is not to control every thought that pops into your head. The key is to take control of your *dominant* thoughts – the thoughts that consume most of your mental energy. This requires focusing on thoughts about what we want in our lives and quickly banishing the thoughts about what we don't want. Of course, you may still be asking, "How do I do that?"

Fortunately, Dr. Bohm left us a wonderful clue in the last line of his quote from the previous chapter: "Our **questions** determine our answers." Think about it. Aren't most of your thoughts framed in the form of questions?

For instance, let's suppose you are driving. While you are driving, you are continually thinking about the task of driving. Sure, you may be thinking of other things as well, but at least part of your brain is working on the problem of safely navigating your car. The way your mind does this is to ask questions: "Is that car ahead slowing down? Do I need to slow down too? Is that car coming over into my lane? Can I get over in time to take the next off-ramp? Did I leave the garage door open?" And the questions never end until you get to your destination, at which point, an entire new set of questions start.

In many ways, the process of thinking is simply the process of asking and answering questions. Remember the GIGO principle? If you ask bad questions, then you get bad answers and, as a result, a bad reality. The quality of your dash basically comes down to the quality of the questions you ask yourself on a daily basis.

ASK BETTER QUESTIONS

Although this may seem like a radical concept, it's actually well established. In fact, our legal system has recognized this concept for centuries. As a result, lawyers are not allowed to ask questions in certain ways because the form of the question will often dictate the answer. For instance, let's suppose a lawyer cross-examines a witness and asks, "So, you say you saw my client commit the crime. Well, I just have one question for you. Are you blind or just plain crazy?" This type of question is objectionable because it only allows the witness to answer the question in a way that discredits him.

How many times have you cross-examined yourself? How many times have you asked yourself a question that didn't have a good answer? We've all done it. In school, I would score poorly on a test and ask myself, "Am I stupid or just lazy?" Obviously, there isn't a good answer to a question like that. And for the same reason that it's objectionable in a court of law, it should be objectionable in the court of your mind.

Another way in which we ask bad questions is when we assume facts that are not true. For some people, the moment something goes wrong they ask, "Why does this type of thing always happen to me?" The problem with this question is that it assumes that "this type of thing" always happens to them. It may seldom happen to them. However, they have input that data into their "computer," and it goes to work to explain why these things always happen to them. Answers to these types of questions are never good.

If you find yourself doing this, stop it! Instead, frame your questions in ways that give you the best chance of obtaining a good result. For instance, let's suppose you want a promotion at work. If you ask yourself, "Can I get the promotion?" there is a chance that your brain will say "No." On the other hand, if you ask yourself *How* can I get the promotion?" then it's a different ballgame. The question assumes that you *can* get the raise and allows your brain to focus on *how* to make it happen. It's amazing how such a small change can have such a big impact on the answer.

I can tell you from experience that much of the success that I've had in life is the result of the questions I've asked. When others asked, "Will this idea work?" I've asked "How can I translate this idea into a profitable business in the shortest amount of time?" Just a simple change in the question produces a remarkably different result.

In fact, during my incarceration, the ability to ask good questions literally saved my life. In the beginning, I asked myself the typical question – "Why did this happen to me?" As a result, my brain went to work on the answers and the result wasn't pretty. In a very short time, I became depressed and found myself crying uncontrollably in my cell and wishing I would die. It was then that I decided that I would ask better questions.

I transformed that question into several more powerful questions: "What can I learn from this experience? What

things do I need to change about myself to prevent something like this from ever happening again? How can I use
this experience to enrich my life and the lives of others? What
can I start doing TODAY to make this happen?"

Once I was able to start asking better questions, my whole
outlook changed. Instead of focusing on my shortcomings or
the unpleasantness of the experience, I focused on my
strengths and the possibility of using that experience to increase the quality of my life. I spent six or seven hours *every
day* (there are no "weekends" in prison) discovering the keys
of success and happiness. In less than three years, I read more
than 600 books on the subject. I studied the works of ancient masters, as well as those of the current leaders in personal development. I can truly say that instead of merely
serving the time, I made the time serve me. Fortunately, you
don't need to go through such a life-altering experience to
get this skill. You can acquire it by simply changing the questions you ask.

START THE DAY OFF RIGHT

This is why I suggest you create a "Wake-Up Question."
This is a question that you can ask yourself each morning. The
point is to start your day off right. We've all heard that breakfast is the most important meal of the day. Well, consider this
question your mental breakfast. After just a week of reading
your Wake-Up Question, I think you'll agree that the questions you ask yourself make all the difference.

Here are examples of how you can make your questions more empowering:

Why do I never seem to have enough money? How can I
earn and save more money for the things I really want in life?
How can I enjoy myself now at little or no cost?

Bad Question	Good Question
Do I have to do this?	How can I perform this task and have a good time doing it?
Why does this type of thing always happen to me?	What can I learn from this situation so that I never find myself in this situation again?
Why can't I do anything right?	How can I translate the successes in my other areas of life to this one area that seems to be troubling me at the moment?
Why do people treat me like this?	How can I learn to better communicate with people so that my interactions are more mutually satisfying?
Will I ever find my soul mate?	What can I do to find my soul mate and have as much fun as possible during the search?
Why is my life so boring?	What do I really enjoy doing and how can I incorporate that activity into my life more often?
Why do I never seem to have enough money?	How can I earn and save more money for the things I really want in life? How can I enjoy myself now at little or no cost?

Perception is Not Reality

People often say that perception is reality. However, in the wake of the storm concerning Martha Stewart, it should be apparent that perception (particularly, public perception) is anything but reality. Just two years ago, Stewart was the media's idea of the quintessential American businesswoman. She was called a "genius," a "pioneer," and a "role model." Yet, following her conviction, the media began calling her string of other names (none of which has been nearly as flattering).

In just twenty-four months, the public perception of Martha Stewart has been turned completely upside down. Has the "real" Martha Stewart changed so radically during this time period? Of course not. The simple truth of the matter is that public perceptions are almost never accurate. People are either praised or pummeled but almost never are they seen as real, flesh and blood individuals, people with virtues *and* faults.

This is important for each of us to remember because there is a public perception of all of us. Of course, most of us don't have our own television shows, magazines, and publicly traded companies, but we do have a "public." It consists of our friends, our families, our business colleagues, the people with whom we attend church, the members of our country club or social service organization, etc.

Just like the general public, your public has a perception of your abilities, talents, and character. And as you begin to make the most of your DASH, that perception will change. Many of these changes will be positive as people begin to recognize a "new" you. And sadly, some of these changes will be negative. As you become more focused on your destiny, you might appear aloof, selfish, and a "stick in the mud" to some of your old ac-quaintances. Unfortunately, it goes with the territory.

This is why it's critical for you to adopt the philoso-phy of the famous book title by Terry Cole-Whitaker, *What You Think about Me is None of My Business*, because it isn't. Other peoples' opinions of you are just that, *their* opin-ions. The only opinion of you that matters is your own. You must never confuse the real you—the one that is destined for greatness—with your public perception. If you do, the results can be disastrous.

This is something I know about firsthand. As a child, the perception of my teachers and classmates was that I was a loser. As I've said many times before, my high school guidance counselor labeled me "Most Likely Not to Succeed." For the first few years of my adult life, I as-sumed the role that others defined for me. As a result, I floated from dead-end job to dead-end job, accomplish-ing little. Fortunately, one day, I had the good fortune to meet a person who saw something in me at a time when I didn't see it in myself. Over time, my own perception of my abilities changed and my life was changed forever.

Therefore, by all means, don't let the perceptions of others keep you from having the life you deserve. It does-n't matter if your friends doubt your ability to complete a marathon or not. Likewise, it doesn't matter if your boss and coworkers don't believe you can lead the company in sales. Nor does it matter whether anyone believes in your ability to start a business, write a bestseller or make enough money in real estate to retire by forty. The only thing that matters is that you think you can do it and that you go out and prove yourself right.

On the other side of the coin, it's important not to take too much stock in the good opinion of others. Inter-estingly, almost as many people are hurt by the good opinions of others as by bad opinions. If you happen to be surrounded by supportive and nurturing people, then consider yourself blessed. However, their high opinion of you isn't enough to make your dreams a reality. That's going to require hard work and persistence on your part.

Sadly, we've all witnessed what happens when people substitute the praise of others for hard work. They become like the star athlete who signs a big contract only to never again perform at the same level again. Remember, your public perception is usually based on your past performance but your ultimate success in life is based on your present and future performance. Therefore, you must be mindful not to let the praise of others go to your head.

Of course, the easiest way to prevent this from happening is to pay little attention to your fans and critics (and yes, you will have both). When your fans begin to sing your praises, don't hire an orchestra and rent out Carnegie Hall. Instead, just hum along as you continue your work. Likewise, when your critics begin to boo and hiss, don't hang your head and walk away in shame. Instead, hold your chin up, stand tall, and resolve that you will ride out this wave of negative public perception. Remember, the only perception of you that can sink your dreams is your own.

"Patterning your life around other's opinions is nothing more than slavery."

Lawana Blackwellde

THOUGHTS FOR YOUR DASH

Determination
> "Courage and perseverance have a magical talisman, before which difficulties disappear and obstacles vanish into air."
>> JOHN QUINCY ADAMS

Attitude
> "I am still determined to be cheerful and happy, in whatever situation I may be; for I have also learned from experience that the greater part of our happiness or misery depends upon our dispositions and not upon our circumstances."
>> MARTHA WASHINGTON

Success
> "If your success is not on your own terms, if it looks good to the world but does not feel good in your heart, it is not success at all."
>> ANNA QUINDLEN

Happiness
> "Only one thing has to change for us to know happiness in our lives: where we focus our attention."
>> GREG ANDERSON

CHAPTER 10

Believing is Seeing

As you pursue your mission in life, you will encounter a number of obstacles. You will experience rejection, setbacks and betrayals. At some point in your quest, you may even run out of money or run out of time. However, none of these obstacles can stop you if you truly *believe* you can do it. Jon Erickson once said:

"I found that I could find the energy ... that I could find the determination to keep on going. I learned that your mind can amaze your body, if you just keep telling yourself, I can do it ... I can do it ... I can do it!"

PLACEBOS AND NOCEBOS

I know this seems simplistic, but it's true. In fact, the power of belief has been *scientifically* demonstrated time after time. In every clinical drug trial, a certain percentage of the patients will respond positively to treatment, even if they are given nothing more than a sugar pill. These people input into their minds that they will be healed and their brains go to work on the result, even without the aid of modern medicine.

Because of the placebo effect, all clinical drug trials now contain at least two groups of patients, one of which does not receive any "real" drugs. Researchers then compare the results of the groups to determine the effectiveness of the drug. This is standard medical procedure and just about everyone acknowledges the placebo effect even if we don't fully know how to explain it.

> **"Drugs are not always necessary, [but] belief in recovery always is."**
> **—Norman Cousins**

However, what isn't commonly known is that there is a "nocebo effect," as well. In a clinical trial for a chemotherapy drug, the patients were sorted into two groups – one group received the chemotherapy drug and a second group received a placebo. After a few weeks, an amazing thing occurred. One-third of patients who received the "fake" chemotherapy began to lose their hair. And none of them had been exposed to any of the harmful effects of chemotherapy. They lost their hair for no other reason than because they *thought* they would. And this result has been duplicated in a number of other clinical trials.

THE FOUR MINUTE MILE

Another amazing story illustrating the power of belief involves the legendary runner Roger Bannister. Bannister was the first man to run a mile in less than four minutes. Before his run, some scientists believed that it was physically impossible for a man to run a sub 4-minute mile. Obviously Bannister believed differently. But that's not the end of the story. Bannister's belief not only changed his performance, but also the performance of thousands of other runners.

Within just one month of Bannister's historic run, 10 other runners broke the 4-minute barrier. Within a year, 37 other runners had broken the mark. And within two years, *300* runners had done it. It took almost 5,000 years of recorded history for one man to run a mile in less than 4 minutes, but just one year for an additional 300 people to do it. This is because once people saw Bannister break the barrier, they believed it was possible for them, too. What was once a human impossibility became an everyday occurrence.

One of the most interesting aspects of this story is that Roger Bannister was not the greatest runner of his day. Once he broke the barrier, there were other men who soon surpassed him. However, Roger Bannister made a name for himself that will not only endure in the annals of sports, but also in history. This is because Bannister possessed a rare insight. While most of the world lives by the saying, "I'll believe it when I see it," Bannister knew that the truth was exactly the opposite – you will see it when you believe it.

THE POWER OF FAITH

It all comes down to faith. Normally, we associate faith with religious or supernatural matters but faith is a big part of everyday life. We all demonstrate a remarkable amount of faith everyday.

Faith in Others

Whenever you get on an airplane, you literally put your life in the hands of complete strangers. You take it on faith that the airline has hired competent pilots and that they have maintained the aircraft properly. In fact, I'd be willing to bet that you've never once asked to see the pilot's license or to take "a peek under the hood" of the aircraft. Instead, we simply put our faith in the airline to do these things for us.

When you think about it, it's lot of faith to put in the

hands of the airline. After all, airlines don't always hire competent people nor do they always maintain their equipment properly. As a result, each year, hundreds of people lose their lives in airplane crashes. So why do we put such blind faith in complete strangers? Because it's necessary if we want to travel a great distance quickly.

For instance, if you want to travel from New York to Los Angeles, then the most efficient way to travel is by airplane. However, you don't *have to* fly. You could always take a bus or a train. However, you would then have to put your faith in the bus or train line that they hire competent people and keep the equipment in proper working order.

On the other hand, you could simply choose to drive yourself across the country. However, even that will require faith in others. On your cross-country drive, you will be sharing the highways with thousands of other drivers, each of whom you will have to trust not to collide into you. Moreover, you will have to trust that all the roads have been maintained in drivable condition. In short, you can't travel any real distance without putting a great deal of faith in others.

Your journey to your mission in life will be the same way. If you will be supplying a product or service, you will have to trust your vendors, supplies, manufacturers, distributors and a host of other parties. Also, depending upon the magnitude of your dream, you may have to trust your financial backers, bankers, lawyers, accountants and other professionals. However, the person you must have the most faith in is *you*.

Faith in You

Remember, this is *your* dream. Others may share it. Others may even help you to attain it but in the final analysis, it's up to you. And the first issue that you must resolve within yourself is that you can do it. And I mean you must really know – not guess and not hope – but *know*. Please note that you don't have to *know* how you are going to do it. You simply need to know that you *can* do it, you deserve it, and that you will get it. Henry David Thoreau said:

"If one advances confidently in the direction of his dreams, and endeavors to live the life which he has imagined, he will meet with a success unexpected in common hours. He will put some things behind, will pass an invisible boundary; new, universal, and more liberal laws will begin to establish themselves around and within him; or the old laws be expanded, and interpreted in his favor in a more liberal sense, and he will live with the license of a higher order of beings."

You must have the quiet self-confidence that comes from knowing you can handle any obstacle that comes in your path. How much do you trust yourself? The answer should be "a lot." Think back to all of the things you've accomplished in life. As a child, you learned to walk, talk, tie your shoes, ride a bike and much more. Of course, you may be thinking, "What's the big deal with that?" Well, just ask a child who cannot do those things, and I'm sure they could tell you.

As an adult, you've probably learned to drive a car, hold down a job, care for your family and so much more. If you currently work for someone else, just think of the faith they place in you. They may trust you to operate equipment worth thousands of dollars. Or perhaps they trust you to negotiate transactions worth thousands (if not millions). Or maybe you're in a management position, where your bosses not only trust you to do your job, but they have also made you responsible for others.

> **"I know God will not give me anything I can't
> handle. I just wish that He didn't trust me so
> much."**
> **—Mother Teresa**

The point is that you are trustworthy. Sure, you aren't perfect. You may have some bad habits. You may even be downright flaky at times, but you have the ability to do wonders. Knowing this fact about yourself is crucial in accomplishing your mission in life.

Words Have Power!

More than four centuries ago, William Shakespeare penned the now famous phrase, "What's in a name? That which we call a rose by any other word would smell as sweet." And although I am reluctant to question perhaps the greatest single figure in English literature, I must take exception with the Bard on this point. What's in a name? Everything!

Words are powerful. Or to quote another great British poet, "The pen is mightier than the sword." The names you give to the things in your life have a direct correlation to the level of success you will enjoy. If you describe your life in positive terms, you will generally experience positive results. On the other hand, if you describe your life in negative terms, you will experience just the opposite. In a very real sense, your vocabulary determines your success in life.

For example, the man who refers to his wife as the "nag" gets a nagging wife and all the misery that goes with it. On the other hand, the man who describes his wife's persistent reminders as "helpful observations" gets just that, helpful observations that generally enhance the quality of his life. Likewise, the woman who describes her husband as "controlling and manipulative" lives under the weight of a dictator. On the other hand, the woman who describes her husband as a "take charge kind of guy" enjoys the benefits of being with someone who knows where they're going and how to get there.

As with anything in life, it's all a matter of perspective. And your perspective is directly tied to the words you use to describe something. For instance, if you were describing yourself to a new employer, would you describe yourself as being "determined" or as being "obsessed"? In a sense, both words mean the same thing—that you are fully committed to achieving your objective regardless of the obstacles. However, describing yourself as "determined" would give you a much better chance of selling yourself to a potential employer.

Of course, advertisers realize the power of words in selling products. You'll never find an advertiser describing its products as "cheap." Instead, they are "inexpensive" or a "tremendous value." Well, the same process occurs each day in the world outside of Madison Avenue. We are constantly selling people on our concepts, ideas, and even ourselves and our greatest tool in this quest is a positive vocabulary. This is particularly true when you are trying to sell to your most important client—you.

To make your DASH all that it can be, you are going to need many great things going for you, the most important of which is a belief in yourself. You need to believe that you are smart enough, talented enough, strong enough, and deserving enough to enjoy the best of what life has to offer. In other words, you need to be "sold" on you and your potential for greatness. Obviously, positive words increase your chances of making this all-important sale and negative words have just the opposite effect.

Therefore, it's important to be vigilant about your vocabulary. This is particularly true when describing your opportunities (less enlightened people call them "problems"). Often, the biggest so-called "problems" present the greatest opportunities for us to stretch and grow. In fact, often without these problems, we would never become even half of what we are capable of being.

In my life, this has certainly been true. If not for my opportunity to spend three years in prison, you would not be reading this newsletter now. I would not have written the DASH book or starting DASH Systems, LLC. In fact, if not for the "problem" of being arrested and sentenced to prison, I truly believe that my past lifestyle would have killed me by now.

And although your "opportunities" may not have been as life changing, you've probably had your share of problems that later turned into great opportunities. For example, perhaps you were fired from a job, only to land in a job with a stronger company and greater upward mobility. Or perhaps you were dumped by a former girlfriend or boyfriend, allowing you to meet your "soul mate." Or perhaps, a change in the economy forced you out of one industry and into a far more lucrative industry with greater long-term prospects.

It's been said many times that problems are opportunities in disguise. Yet, we often allow ourselves to be blinded by the labels we place on situations. For instance, we label our opportunity to seek out new employment as a "layoff." As a result, we spend so much time focusing on being "off" the last job that we don't take advantage of the opportunity to get "on" a better employment track. The same applies to the opportunities that arise from the other "problems" we all encounter from time to time.

The bottom line is that words have power. They affect the perception that others have of you and more importantly, they affect your self-image. Words even affect your ability to seize the opportunities in your DASH. To turn a familiar phrase, "Sticks and stones may break your bones but the right words will always help you."

"Our subconscious minds have no sense of humor, play no jokes, and cannot tell the difference between reality and an imagined thought or image. What we continually think about eventually will manifest in our lives."

Sidney Madwed

THOUGHTS FOR YOUR DASH

Determination
> "It sometimes seems that we have only to love a
> thing greatly to get it."
>
> ROBERT COLLIER

Attitude
> "We cannot always control our thoughts, but we
> can control our words."
>
> FLORENCE SCOVEL SHINN

Success
> "The conditions of conquest are always easy. We
> have but to toil awhile, endure awhile, believe al-
> ways, and never turn back."
>
> MARCUS ANNAEUS SENECA

Happiness
> "The happiest and most contented people are
> those who each day perform to make the best of
> their abilities."
>
> ALFRED A. MONTAPERT

CHAPTER 11

Tapping Into Your True Strength

The most powerful part of your mind is the subconscious mind. Consider that we are only consciously aware of a small portion of the activities going on in our brains. For instance, your heart has beaten approximately 55,000 times in the last 24 hours. How many of those beats did you consciously cause? How many times did you intentionally breathe or blink your eyes today? The answer is that you had no conscious part in these activities. Your brain works on autopilot 24 hours of every day, performing all the vital functions necessary to keep you alive. But your subconscious mind also handles many of the routine aspects of your day.

THE POWER OF HABITS

In fact, most of your habits are controlled by your subconscious mind. Think about it. If you are a person who fidgets, taps pencils on your desk, chews pens or engages in other similar behavior, do you do it consciously? Chances are that you don't even realize you're doing it most of the time, because it's just a habit. However, don't underestimate the power of habits. According to Mahatma Gandhi, "Our thoughts create our words, our words create our beliefs, our beliefs create our habits, our habits create our destiny."

I can tell you from experience that this is true, particularly with respect to mental habits. When I was younger, I often found myself feeling frustrated and hopeless. I met with failure at every turn. At one point, I wanted to give up completely. I was ready to accept a mediocre and unhappy life because I was tired of setting myself up for failure.

My problems largely resulted from my habitual unconscious (or subconscious) internal dialogue. Whenever I was confronted with a challenge, my mind would run a script that said: "What are you doing? You mess everything up. You fail at everything. You know you can't do this. You're only going to fail, so why try to begin? Stick with what you have and be happy with it."

Is it any wonder that I failed? Although, on a conscious level, I thought I wanted success, my subconscious mind was focused only on what I couldn't do and how foolish it was to try anything at all. As we've discussed earlier, thoughts (even subconscious ones) are things and my reality reflected my dominant thoughts. Therefore, my thoughts of inadequacy resulted in damaging internal dialogue, which in turned resulted in my belief of failure, which in turn formed habits of failure, which in turn formed a destiny of failure.

> **"The chains of habit are usually too small to be felt until they are too strong to be broken."**
> **—Samuel Johnson**

This cycle started changing for me only when I changed the internal dialogue. I replaced it with a new, empowering message: "You can do this. If someone else has done it and succeeded, then you can too. The reward of success is well worth the work and sacrifice. You will learn from each failure and eventually succeed." This new dialogue created excitement in my life and more importantly, it created positive results.

Are you the victim of similar negative self-talk? If you answered "no," don't be so sure. This type of internal conversation could be a habit that, like biting your fingernails, you may not even notice.

AFFIRMATIONS

This is why I suggest that you develop an affirmation you can consciously feed to your subconscious mind every day. And, just as with any other "food," I suggest you give yourself a regular diet of three healthy affirmations per day. In fact, if it makes it easier for you, schedule them around mealtime. Use the affirmation above if you like, but your affirmation will probably be more powerful if it's something you create for yourself.

I understand that some of you may have an aversion to affirmations. For some reason, affirmations have gotten a bum rap over the years. This is largely because some people have magical expectations of affirmations. A positive affirmation is nothing more than a mental bath. It scrubs your mind of negative thoughts.

Freshen Up

However, as with any bath, affirmations are limited in three respects. For one, even the most thorough bath won't last forever. Think about it. A good, long bath or shower will last you 24 hours *at best*. And this assumes that you don't move around much in those 24 hours. This is why I suggest that you say your affirmation three times a day to help "freshen up" your mental attitude.

121

Keep Clean

Second, you won't stay "clean" after a bath if you immediately jump into a puddle of mud. Some people think they can say a quick affirmation and then hang out with negative people or watch negative television programs and remain "inspired." It just doesn't work that way.

The sad truth is that we live in a negative world. As a result, positive words become even more important. According to one legend, an ancient man visited Sodom before its destruction. He walked around the town, trying to talk the people into changing their ways, but no one would listen. He then began carrying a sign that read "Repent," but no one paid attention to that either. Finally, he began running through the streets, yelling, "Repent! Repent! What you are doing is wrong! It will kill you!" Once again, no one paid him much attention.

Finally, a local man stopped him and asked, "Can't you see that no one is listening to you?" The man replied, "Yes, I can see that!" The local man was confused by this answer and asked, "So why on earth do you continue?" The man replied, "When I first arrived at this city, I was convinced I could change them. Now, I continue shouting so that they don't change me." This ancient man understood that we are all susceptible to the negative influences around us, so he continued to preach his message, if only to himself.

Perhaps an even better metaphor would be to compare an affirmation with exercising at the gym. Do you think you could get into shape by working out one day and then being done with it? Of course not. However, how about if you worked out everyday religiously but then went home and ate a gallon of ice cream, a dozen doughnuts and a bucket of fried chicken? Would this get you into shape? The answer is "yes" but only if the shape you were going for was round. The point is that affirmations are effective but only if performed regularly and in conjunction with other helpful mental activities.

There Are No Guarantees

Third, affirmations do <u>not</u> guarantee success. In fact, there are no guarantees for success. Sometimes you will win and sometimes you will lose. It's that simple. However, by feeding positive thoughts into your subconscious mind, your winning percentage will increase. In fact, affirmations literally saved my life.

When I first got to prison, I wondered how I would survive the ordeal of being away from everything and everyone I loved. I used the following affirmation to boost my spirits and keep me sane:

Things may not seem to be working out for me right now but I know that I will make the best of the situation. I know that I will do everything that I can, one day at a time. I will get through this as a winner. I will not worry but rather look at what I am going through as a challenge: a time to develop patience and self-confidence and realize that I can change my attitude even if I can't change my circumstances. I am a survivor! I am going to handle this. I am going to find strength I didn't know I had. Soon enough, I will be on the other side and I will look back on this time and draw strength and courage from the fact that even though the road was rocky, I made it through and carried on.

VISUALIZATIONS

Another helpful exercise is to visualize your future success. Take time each day to close your eyes and see yourself doing whatever it is that you wish to be doing. If you want to take your family to Disney World, visualize arriving at the Magic Kingdom, being greeted by Mickey and Minnie Mouse, riding the Matterhorn and visiting Epcot Center. Likewise, if you want to become a pop singer, picture yourself in the recording studio, on stage at a concert, and on the platform accepting a Grammy.

You may think this is silly, but trust me – all peak performers visualize their performance beforehand. Have you ever noticed how long Olympic divers stand on the diving board with their eyes closed? You don't think they are up there taking quick catnaps, do you? Of course not! They are visualizing *in detail* the dive they are about to perform.

I do the same thing before I give a speech. I spend a great amount of time preparing the quotes, the stories and the jokes in my talks but I always spend some time visualizing my performance, too. I see myself on the platform, speaking clearly and with power to a wide-eyed audience. I see the audience clapping when I make a profound point and laughing when I make a joke. In my mind's eye, when I tell a touching story, grown men weep in the aisles. At the end of my speech, I visualize the audience erupting into a 20-minute standing ovation in which the crowd shouts, "Encore! Encore! Encore!" Sometimes, I even visualize the crowd rioting when told that I won't come out for a *fifth* curtain call.

Visualizations will not only help you to reach peak performance, but they will also help you persevere when things look bleak. One reason people give up on their dreams is because they get to a point where they can't "see" their way to success. In fact, scientists illustrated this point in an experiment with laboratory rats.

They took one rat and dropped it into a jar of water and then placed the jar in complete darkness. The rat continued to swim for about three minutes before giving up and allowing itself to drown. They then took a second rat and dropped it into a jar of water. However, this time, they allowed a tiny ray of light to shine into the jar. As a result, the second rat continued to swim for thirty-six hours until finally rescued. That tiny ray of hope was enough to keep the rat alive for more than a day while the first rat perished in *minutes*.

As long as we can see a light at the end of the tunnel, we will continue to struggle through the murky waters of life. Therefore, whenever you face a hurdle that seems too high to conquer, try visualizing yourself clearing the hurdle with ease.

Remember the TITO principle – treasure in, treasure out. And, the more specific you make your visualizations, the more opportunity you give your subconscious mind to work filling in the details. So load up on the mental treasures. After all, they're free!

LOOK BACK

It's also necessary to take a look back to see how far you've come. If you've set a big goal for yourself, it may still be in the distance. If so, you can get discouraged chasing a dream on the horizon unless you take a look in the rearview mirror to see how far you've come. For instance, let's suppose your goal is to create a worldwide charitable organization and right now, you're still operating out of a small office building in your town. Well, take a look back and remember how it was when you were operating out of your garage. Remember in detail the dust, the motor oil stains in the middle of your "office" and the fact that you didn't have heat in the winter or air conditioning in the summer. Thinking about your progress can be a great energy boost for the next leg of your dash.

SEEK INSPIRATION

It's also important to surround yourself with inspirational messages. Buy a calendar that has a new inspirational saying each day. Post motivating quotes and pictures on the walls of your home and office. Read success stories. The library is filled with biographies of men and women who have done extraordinary things.

Choose entertainment that is inspiring, too. Listen to music that is inspiring, like the theme from *Rocky* or *Chariots of Fire*. In short, bombard your mind with so much positive input that it can't produce negative output.

BE OPTIMISTIC

Perhaps most importantly, strive to be an optimist. Choose to see the glass as half full, rather than half empty. This isn't always easy but it's certainly worth it. Having a positive mental attitude will allow you to do everything better than if you had a negative mental attitude.

One way to accomplish this is to the use the power of questions. Whenever something "bad" happens, ask the question: "What's good about this situation?" There will be times where you won't be able to think of a single positive thing. However, your subconscious mind can, and will, if you keep asking the question. It's just a matter of putting that billion dollar brain to work for you instead of against you.

I Want to Be Like Maria

A few months ago, I received an e-mail from a fellow DASHer and thought it might inspire you as much as it inspired me. This e-mail was somewhat different from the many e-mails I gladly receive each week from those of you who are successfully implementing the DASH Principles because the subject of this e-mail, Maria, is not a DASH reader. In fact, from what I could gather, Maria has never heard of the DASH book. Yet, she embodies the DASH Principles better than almost anyone I've ever read about.

Maria is a recent immigrant who currently works as a housekeeper for the person who wrote me the e-mail. At night, Maria attends school and is working toward her degree. Well, as the story was told, one day, Maria was late for work. This was unusual, prompting her employer to become somewhat concerned. Fortunately, about twenty minutes later, Maria arrived, along with her six-year-old son. Upon entering the home, Maria immediately began to apologize for her tardiness and explained that her car wouldn't start that morning.

"Well, how did you get here?" asked her friend and employer. Maria answered matter-of-factly, "We walked." "You walked? You live at least six miles from here!" exclaimed her amazed employer. Maria simply answered, "Sí," and began her daily chores. Needless to say, Maria's employer was blown away that a woman would walk six miles with a young child in tow just to get to work.

And quite frankly, so was I. In fact, I was humbled by Maria's commitment to meeting her obligations. I'd like to think that I would have done the same thing in that situation, but honestly, I'm not so sure. As I think back on it, there have been many times when I didn't meet my commitments and I could have done so with a lot less effort than Maria expended to meet hers. And if you're honest, you can probably say the same thing.

Just think, by most people's standards, Maria had enough of a reason to miss work that day. Yet, Maria understood that although there may be 10,000 reasons for failing to meet your commitments, there is never a single excuse. Therefore, she decided that she was going to go to work *no matter what*. And in doing so, she not only inspired her employer, she inspired me and hopefully now you, but she has taken a huge step toward obtaining her piece of the American Dream.

Although I gave up gambling years ago, I'd be willing to come out of "retirement" to bet that Maria *will* finish school. I'd also be willing to bet that she will succeed in whatever field she enters. Why? Because she has a "no matter what" attitude. She will succeed no matter what the obstacles. If only we were all like Maria.

Well, the good news is that we can be just like her. We simply need to throw away our excuses and decide, once and for all, that we will meet our commitments *no matter what*. If we promise our boss that the report will be ready by Friday, then it will be ready by Friday *no matter what*. If we promise our family a vacation to Hawaii next summer, then they will be sitting on those white-sand beaches sipping mai tais *no matter what*.

If we do anything less, then we do a disservice to those who put their trust in us. And perhaps, equally important, we do a disservice to ourselves. Every time, we make a promise that we don't keep, we weaken our own credibility. It doesn't take long before people stop trusting you altogether. Sure, you may be reliable 90 percent of the time, but who wants to hope and pray that they don't fall in the unlucky 10 percent category?

And take it from me; your credibility is all you've got. I learned this lesson the hard way. My unwillingness to meet my commitments to investors and customers lead to my incarceration. However, believe it or not, my freedom was not the biggest casualty in this situation. After all, in a little more than three years, I was released from prison. Yet, my reputation is still shackled to the misdeeds of my past. Despite the fact that I have committed my life to helping others make the most of their lives, there are still some people who will *never* trust me as far as they can throw me (which isn't far, considering I'm 6'4" and weigh 220 pounds).

Therefore, before you do irreparable harm to your reputation in the eyes of your family members, friends, colleagues, and peers, learn to be a "no matter what" person. Resolve within yourself that you are going to meet your commitments regardless of the circumstances that may arise to seemingly "excuse" you from doing so. When people know beyond a shadow of a doubt that they can count on you, you will be amazed at the opportunities that open up to you. Your customers will entrust you with larger orders. Your clubs and organizations will entrust you with greater positions. And your family and friends will respect and appreciate you more than ever.

For instance, can you imagine the respect that Maria will receive from her young son? Perhaps, today, he can't appreciate why his mommy made him walk such a long way but one day, he will. And he will be proud to be Maria's son and hopefully, want to be just like her.

As a relatively young man, I had the opportunity to play golf with Michael Jordan on a few occasions. As you can imagine, I was honored to be in the presence of perhaps the greatest athlete of our time. And like almost everyone else, I wanted to be like Mike. And although I certainly still have a lot of respect for Mr. Jordan, I now want to be like Maria. And I will be like Maria...NO MATTER WHAT!

"Do all the good you can, by all the means you can, in all the ways you can, in all the places you can, at all the times you can, to all the people you can, as long as ever you can."

John Wesley

THOUGHTS FOR YOUR DASH

Determination
> "A determined soul will do more with a rusty monkey wrench than a loafer will accomplish with all the tools in a machine shop."
>> ROBERT HUGHES

Attitude
> "First say to yourself what you would be; and then do what you have to do."
>> EPICTETUS

Success
> "I've always made a total effort, even when the odds seemed entirely against me. I never quit trying; I never felt that I didn't have a chance to win."
>> ARNOLD PALMER

Happiness
> "Action may not always bring happiness; but there is no happiness without action."
>> BENJAMIN DISRAELI

Part Three

SUCCESS

"Success is how high you bounce after you
have fallen."
—Eric J. Aronson

CHAPTER 12

Acting the Part

Belief is the starting point of all achievement. Without a belief in your mission and in yourself, you can *never* succeed on a long-term basis. You may have temporary success, but eventually the supercomputer between your ears will work to sabotage your success.

Remember, the three step process is to be, then to do and finally, to have. As we move forward, I want you to be mindful of your mental state. Is your internal dialogue nurturing your dream, or is it toxic? Are you surrounding yourself with people, images and words that support your growth or with those that are suffocating it? These are important things you should ask yourself regularly.

YOU MUST TAKE ACTION

But let's not kid ourselves here. Positive thinking alone is not enough. You must also take action. As one speaker says, "You can't make footprints in the sands of time while sitting on your butt. And who wants to make butt prints in the sands of time?"

We all know people who are currently making butt prints

in the sands of time. They have lots of dreams and ambitions, but unfortunately none of it is accompanied by any real action. They talk about what they are going to do when they finally get their last degree or move to the day shift or get enough money together or whatever the excuse is this week.

The unfortunate truth is that many people have their *wishbone* where their backbone should be. All the "wouldas, couldas and shouldas" in the world will not get a single thing done. As Nolan Bushell, the founder of Atari said:

"A lot of people have ideas, but there are few who decided to do something about them now. Not tomorrow. Not next week. But today. The true entrepreneur is a doer, not a dreamer."

GET IN THE GAME

You've probably heard the story of the good and faithful man who fell on hard times. He seemed to encounter one financial disaster after another. One night in desperation, he prayed, "Dear God, please let me win the lottery!" At first, he was optimistic that God would grant his wish. However, after not winning for several months, his faith began to falter. After a year, he became downright bitter.

In anger, he shouted at the heavens, "God, I believed you would help me, yet an entire year has passed without you answering my prayers!" At that moment, lightning flashed and thunder rolled and a voice bellowed from the heavens, "Give me a break up here! The least you could do is buy a ticket!"

Have you bought your ticket? Have you taken a chance on yourself? And that doesn't mean you have to quit your job, sell your home and sink your life savings into a new business tomorrow. But it does mean that you have to start where you are, with what you have and do *something*.

FIRE, READY, AIM!

Sometimes we have a tendency to wait until we've figured out every little detail or, as they say, until we "get our ducks in a row." Well, ducks are not that cooperative. Your ducks are not going to line up in a row for you. You are going to have to take your first steps while your ducks are scattered everywhere. You can't sit on the sidelines of life, waiting for everything to be "just right."

There is a fable that illustrates this point. In this fable, a group of animals and insects decided to play a football game. On one team were the larger animals – bears, elephants and tigers. And on the other team were the smaller animals – rabbits, squirrels and insects.

Well, as you can imagine, the larger animals jumped out to an early lead. By halftime, the score was 119-0. The smaller animals had not mustered much offense and hadn't made a single tackle on defense. However, all of this changed in the second half. In fact, whether the bear ran up the middle or the cheetah swept to the outside, it was tackled instantly by the centipede. Despite the great performance, the smaller animals were not able to surmount the big first half lead and eventually lost the game.

In the losing locker room, the rabbit approached the centipede and said, "You were incredible out there in the second half! But where were you in the first half when they were scoring at will?" The centipede replied, "I was tying my shoes!"

Many people are just like the centipede. They spend so much time getting ready for the big game of life that, by the time they get into the game, it's half over and the outcome has been decided. Sometimes, we simply have to leap into action with our shoes untied. As Henry David Thoreau once said, "We must walk consciously only part way toward our goal, and then leap in the dark to our success."

Thoreau was right. Unless you only have a short distance to travel in your dash, it's going to be impossible to precisely map out your route from where you are to where you want to go. There are simply too many variables to compute. The key is to get started on your mission today.

INSPIRATION FOLLOWS ACTION

Sometimes we allow ourselves to be held back by the thought that we don't *feel* like acting right now. This is particularly true of people with creative talents, like writers and artists. They often wait for the inspiration to hit them. However, the truth is that action does not follow inspiration but rather inspiration follows action. Musical historian Ernest Newman said:

"The great composer does not set to work because he is inspired but becomes inspired because he is working. Beethoven, Bach, Mozart settled down day after day to the job at hand with as much regularity as an accountant settles down each day to his figures. They didn't waste time waiting for inspiration."

The same principle works in relationships. No matter how wonderful the relationship, there are going to be days when you don't "feel" loving towards the other person. Enough of those days can spell disaster for the relationship. When you hear people talk about these situations, they say things like "we simply fell out of love." However, these people don't understand that love isn't a feeling; love is an action. And as with other actions, you don't wait until you feel loving feelings to act, you act and then wait for the loving feelings.

For instance, a man once walked into the office of a divorce lawyer. "I've had it! I want a divorce," he said. When the lawyer asked why, the man explained that his wife had grown fat and lazy over the years and that he could no longer stand her nagging. As they discussed the logistics of the divorce, the lawyer could tell that the husband not only wanted a divorce, but he also wanted to hurt his wife.

So the lawyer said, "Hey! I have an idea! Instead of divorcing your wife immediately, go home and treat her like a queen for a few months. Buy her flowers. Make her breakfast in bed. Take her on a vacation. That way, when you finally dump her, she will be *devastated*." The man agreed that it was a great plan and left the lawyer's office.

Two months later, the lawyer called the man and said, "Your divorce papers are ready. When do you want to come in and sign them?" The man replied, "Are you kidding? You expect me to divorce the sexiest, kindest and most loving woman I've ever known?" By treating his wife as a "queen," the man was finally able to see her majestic qualities. Remember, the inspiration follows action and not vice versa.

THE POWER OF MOMENTUM

There is real power in just getting started. In fact, momentum is one of the strongest forces on the planet. For instance, a standing locomotive can be held in place by a small block of wood. However, once that same locomotive gains momentum, it can crash through a solid brick wall – it becomes unstoppable. You are the same way. As soon as you get momentum behind your actions, you too will be unstoppable.

It's All Smooth Sailing

Recently, a friend of mine asked, "How can you be so positive all the time? Don't you ever have a bad day?" I had to confess that I have many bad days. In fact, I informed my friend that I was having a terrible day that day. Yet, I had to remind my friend that I don't judge my life on the basis of one day. I judge how well I am doing by looking at the big picture.

I learned this lesson as a young stockbroker. When I would first invest in a stock, I would watch that stock like a hawk. If it went up that day, I would be excited. On the other hand, if it went down, I'd get depressed. Well, it took a little while, but eventually, I learned that you can't judge an investment by its performance on a particular day. Even the best investments can lose money on a given day. The key to judging an investment is to look at its performance over time.

Well, the same is true in judging your performance toward your goals. You can't judge how well you're doing as a salesperson, entrepreneur, or a parent by the results of a single day. You're simply not going to make the sale, turn a profit, or say all the right things every day. The best you can you hope for is that, through all the peaks and valleys, your stock will steadily rise over time.

Yet, too many people miss the peaks of success because they are mired in the valleys of failure. For example, when the stock market crashed in 1987, millions of investors sold their holdings and got out of the market. They saw one very bad day in the market and bailed. Yet, had they looked at the big picture, they wouldn't have been so worried. Even with a 508-point drop in a single day, the market was still up over 30 percent for those last two years. And with the economy steaming steadily ahead, the long-term outlook was positive. In fact, it took just fifteen months for the Dow Jones to return to its pre-crash levels. And over the next decade, it more than *quadrupled*. Yet, many people missed out on one of the greatest bull markets of all-time because they let one bad day—November 19, 1987—scare them out of the market.

If you're going to make the most out of this game of life, you can't let a bad day scare you out of the arena. You have to take the long-term view. Sure, today may have been a terrible day, but what about the long-term out-look? How have you been doing over the past six months? What can you expect for the future? When you put your situation into this kind of perspective, does one bad day really matter all that much? It's just one of the valleys you have to go through to get to the next peak.

With this kind of realization, you're unlikely to be rattled and give up on your goal. You're more likely to ride out the highs and lows on your journey to success. And perhaps, equally important, you're far more likely to enjoy the trip. Take it from someone who has experienced some dramatic peaks and valleys, a sense of balance is a key to happiness.

If you allow your mental state to fluctuate with your fortunes on any particular day, you'll be on an emotional roller coaster. Some days, you'll be happy and on top of the world. And other days, you'll be miserable and de-pressed. I don't think that anyone really wants to live in this kind of turmoil. Well, the way to avoid these highs and lows is to smooth out your perspective and take a more long-term view of your circumstances. As Samuel Butler once wrote, "Happiness and misery depend not on how high up or low down you are—they depend not upon these, but on the direction in which you are tending."

"When it comes to happiness, well, sometimes life is just okay, sometimes it's comfortable, sometimes wonderful, sometimes boring,
sometimes unpleasant. When your day's not perfect, it's not a failure or a terrible loss. It's just another day."

Barbara Sher

THOUGHTS FOR YOUR DASH

Determination
> "Everything in life can be nourishing. Everything
> can bless us, but we've got to be there for the
> blessing to occur."
>
> MacRina Wiederkehr

Attitude
> "Finish each day and be done with it.... You have
> done what you could; some blunders and absurdi-
> ties no doubt crept in; forget them as soon as you
> can. Tomorrow is a new day; you shall begin it well
> and serenely."
>
> Ralph Waldo Emerson

Success
> "Yesterday ended last night. Every day is a new be-
> ginning. Learn the skill of forgetting. And move on."
>
> Norman Vincent Peale

Happiness
> "Happiness consists more in small conveniences
> or pleasures that occur every day, than in great
> pieces of good fortune that happen but seldom."
>
> Benjamin Franklin

CHAPTER 13

Time Waits for No One

One of the key characteristics of successful people is that they understand the importance of time. When you really think about it, time is our most precious resource.

THE MOST PRECIOUS RESOURCE ON EARTH

For one, there is a finite amount of it. With every other resource – money, materials or labor – there is an almost inexhaustible supply of it available to us. But there will never be more than 24 hours in a day. In this way, time is the great equalizer. Whether we are rich or poor, tall or short, smart or dumb, skinny or fat, we all get the same amount of time each day. The renowned writer and speaker Percy Whiting said this about time:

"Time is a fixed income and, as with any fixed income, the real problem facing us is how to work successfully with our daily allotment. Plan each day down to the moment because once time is wasted, you can never get it back."

Second, unlike other resources, time can't be conserved. If you don't spend all your money in a given day, then you can put it into a bank account and let it accrue for a rainy day. That doesn't work with time.

You have to *spend* every second of it each day. There simply isn't any way to save time from one day and carry it over to the next. In this sense, there is no such thing as "saving time." In dealing with time, the choice is not whether to save it or spend it, but rather *how* to spend it.

YOUR DAILY ALLOWANCE

One way to think of time is to imagine that each day you are given a bag full of 86,400 coins – one coin for each second of the day. You can spend these coins in any way you wish, but at the end of the day, you must return any un-spent coins. This is a great metaphor because it forces us to really think about how we spend our time.

For instance, if each of your daily coins were worth $1, you'd have $86,400 to spend each day. If you couldn't save any of it for the future, how much of it would you spend each day? As much as you could, right? Well, how much of it would you spend on stuff you really didn't like? As little as you could. Now, are you spending your time this way?

How much of your time are you spending as opposed to just letting it slip through your fingers? At the end of a day, is your bag of coins empty, or are you turning in a bag that is practically full? Of the coins you spend during the day, how many of them are spent to purchase things that *you* really want? Or, are your coins used to purchase things for other people?

Now I'm not suggesting you adopt a hedonistic phi-losophy that requires you to spend every waking moment in the pursuit of your own pleasure. However, *some* of the

86,400 seconds in every day should be devoted to you. The exact percentage is an individual question and is really more about lifestyle choice and balance. Nevertheless, I've found that most people do not *choose* how their time is spent.

How you spend your time is a choice

Instead, this choice is made by their families, their employers and even society. For example, if you work in a traditional job, did you make the choice to spend 40 hours a week at work? Probably not. If you had been given a choice, you may have decided to work 20, 32 or even 58 hours a week instead.

My point is not to get you to walk into work tomorrow and demand that your boss allow you to work one day a week – though if you think you can get away with it, go for it! I want you to simply think about how you spend your time and whether you want to make changes. Would you like to spend more time with your family or volunteering at the local homeless shelter or working on the Great American Novel? If so, it's important to realize that the choice is yours to make.

THE "SOMEDAY WHEN" SYNDROME

It's also important to realize that the time to make that choice is *now*. So many people put off making that choice until some future date. They seem to be suffering from the "Someday When" Syndrome – "Someday when I get married, I'll …" "Someday when I get divorced, I'll …" "Someday when I retire, I'll …" But in many cases, someday never comes. The future isn't promised to any of us. There are no guarantees that there will be a next year, a next month or even a tomorrow for *any* of us.

We all know people who've had their "someday" wiped out by a tragic accident. We also know people who've watched their "someday" eaten away by sudden illness. How many times have you heard the story about the person who finally retires, only to suffer a fatal heart attack just weeks or months into retirement? The key is to turn someday into TODAY.

"Live each day as if it were your last day—someday you'll be right."
—Unknown

The theologian Jonathan Edwards said, "I resolve never to do anything I wouldn't do if it were the last hour of my life." I will be the first to admit that it would be extremely difficult to live your life that way. After all, who would wait in the line at the post office or go to the grocery store in the last hour of their lives? However, the sentiment behind this statement is sincere.

Perhaps a better question to ask is "If I only had six months to live, how would I spend my remaining dash?" Once you've answered this question, I strongly recommend that you start spending as much of your time as possible doing just that. The simple truth is that you may only have six months to live. The late actor Michael Landon, while on his deathbed, expressed this sentiment better than anyone:

"Somebody should tell us, right at the start of our lives, that we are dying. Then we might live life to the limit every minute of every day. 'Do it!' I say. Whatever you want to do, do it now! There are only so many tomorrows."

KILLING PROCRASTINATION

Perhaps the biggest difference between people who are successful and those who aren't is that successful people understand the destructive power of procrastination. In many ways, procrastination is like cancer; it secretly eats away your opportunities until finally it has taken over your life.

After all, when you first put off making a phone call, writing a proposal or conducting research, there are usually no negative side effects. As a result, it becomes that much easier to put off the task the next day. After all, you let it slip yesterday and nothing bad happened; what's going to happen today, right? The answer is usually nothing. However, when you stack enough days like that on top of each other, you reach a point of no return. At this point, you can't act even if you wanted to.

We've all had the experience of meeting someone and telling them about a project and having them say, "That sounds interesting! Give me a call about that sometime." You get their phone number and plan to call them the very next day. However, for some reason, you put it off. You say to yourself, "No problem! I'll do it tomorrow." However, you forget to make the call the next day and the next day and so on. Six months later, you come across this person's phone number while cleaning out your desk. Unfortunately, you've waited too long by this point. You couldn't possibly call the person after six months, as they've probably long forgotten your original conversation. Besides, how are you going to explain not calling?

This is how the cancer of procrastination metastasizes into a deadly tumor and eats away at your opportunity for success. For this reason, procrastination must be diagnosed and cut out of your life. The easiest way to do this is to put off procrastinating. I'm serious. Whenever you feel like putting off a task, do the task and then tell yourself, "I'll start procrastinating tomorrow!" If you are like most of us, you're good at procrastinating – so why not use it in your favor?

ONE BITE AT A TIME

Sometimes we fall prey to the deadly "Someday When" syndrome and the cancer of procrastination because we simply don't know what to do next. This is particularly true when the goal is big and we feel like an ant given the task of eating an elephant. It just looks like too large a task for us to handle. As a result, we become paralyzed with uncertainty and never end up taking any action.

Of course, the way to move beyond this paralysis is to realize that the only way for an ant to eat an elephant (or for you to reach your goal) is to break the job into manageable pieces. Attack the problem one bite at a time, and the project becomes almost easy. For instance, if someone asked you to rip a phone book in half, could you do it all at once? Probably not. However, what if you ripped the book 5 pages at a time? Could you do that? Of course. The key is to break the large task into smaller, bite-size chunks.

So let's suppose you've been telling yourself for years that you need to lose 50 lbs. and get in shape but have been paralyzed by the enormity of the project. In this case, you don't have to redo your entire life to get started on your goal. Instead, you could simply take the first step towards improvement.

Perhaps if you live close enough to work, you could start walking to work instead of driving. Or perhaps, you could start taking the stairs to your floor instead of the elevator. Now, you may say, "But hey, I work on the 60th floor!" In that case, perhaps you could take the elevator to the 55th floor and walk the rest of the way up. The point is to take a relatively small step that will bring you closer to your ultimate goal of losing weight and getting in shape. Over time, you can take more steps in that direction.

In fact, this is how the transcontinental railroad system was built. The introduction of railroads in 1829 made traveling through the interior of America much easier than it had been. From the very early days of the railroad, people envisioned a system where a person could transport cargo to anywhere in the country. But in the beginning, there wasn't sufficient capital to lay the thousands of miles of railroad track the project required.

So did people just give up and go back to their covered wagons? Of course not. They built smaller regional lines that would run between just a few cities. Over time, the profitability of these lines allowed them to add more cities to the route and to connect with other railroads. Finally, the first transcontinental railroad was completed in 1869, just 40 years after its introduction.

So, take a moment to consider your major goals and objectives and determine how they can be broken into bite-size pieces. For instance, let's suppose you want to start a foundation to cure autism. Your first step may be to form a nonprofit corporation. You can further break that step into bite-size pieces – creating a name, downloading the forms from the internet, filling out and mailing the forms, etc. The key is to do something *today* to move you one step closer to your dream. In fact, before we go to bed each evening, we should ponder the words of this poem:

What Have I Done Today?
Anonymous

I shall do so much in the years to come,
But what have I done today?
I shall give my gold in a princely sum,
But what did I give today?
I shall build a mansion in the sky,
But what have I built today?
It's sweet in idle dreams to bask,
But if not I, who shall do the task?
Yes, this is the question each soul must ask:
What have I done today?

Inoculate Yourself Against SWS

This winter, millions of Americans raced to get flu shots. Yet, most of us continue to leave ourselves vulnerable to a far more deadly syndrome. And I'm not referring to SARS. Nor am I referring to AIDS, which kills millions across the globe each year. The syndrome I'm referring to is far more deadly than AIDS because it prevents most of us from ever really living in the first place. The syndrome I'm referring to is the "Someday When..." Syndrome.

You know it. It's the syndrome that causes you to say, "Someday when I have more time, I'm going to finally take my family on that vacation." Or perhaps it causes you to say, "Someday when I have more money, I will give to my favorite charity." Or maybe, "Someday when I have more education or training, I'm going to go after that promotion." The problem with SWS is that it's premised on a lie—the lie of *someday*.

The truth is that you don't have a someday. Someday is not promised to any of us. After all, you probably knew someone who had their someday eaten away in weeks because of an illness or someone who had their someday destroyed in the blink of an eye because of an accident. In fact, on September 11, 2001, nearly 3,000 Americans saw their someday go up in a ball of flames.

On that tragic day, we wept for the husbands who lost wives. We wept for the wives who lost husbands. We wept for the parents who lost children and for the children who lost parents. And we also should have wept for the somedays that were lost.

Someday, someone in the World Trade Center was going to start a homeless shelter that would not only feed the bodies of the homeless but also their minds and spirits. But that someday never came. Someday, someone on one of those planes was going to start a business that would not only provide jobs to thousands but also provide them with homes, cars, and a part of the American Dream. But someday never came. Someday, someone in the Pentagon was going to repair a relationship with a loved one. But someday never came.

There are no guarantees about a someday for any of us. The only day we do have is TODAY. So let's make the most of it. Today, let's do all the things we say we are going to do "someday when...".

THOUGHTS FOR YOUR DASH

Determination
> "The vision must be followed by the venture. It is not enough to stare up the steps—we must step up the stairs."
>
> VANCE HAVNER

Attitude
> "Get excited and enthusiastic about your own dream. This excitement is like a forest fire—you can smell it, taste it, and see it from a mile away."
>
> DENIS WAITLEY

Success
> "The secret of health for both mind and body is not to mourn for the past, worry about the future, or anticipate troubles, but to live in the present moment wisely and earnestly."
>
> BUDDHA

Happiness
> "As you walk down the fairway of life you must smell the roses, for you only get to play one round."
>
> BEN HOGAN

CHAPTER 14

You Do Have the Time

One of the common excuses people give for not pursuing their dreams is that they simply don't have the time. If you have been guilty of using this excuse (and we all have), then stop it! If anyone in the world is doing what you'd love to be doing, then you know that lack of time is not the problem. We all get the same 86,400 seconds per day. Therefore, the problem is not that you don't have the time, but that you haven't spent the time you have on pursuing your dream.

In a nutshell, the problem is never lack of time, but rather lack of time-management *skills*. As legendary business leader Peter Drucker once said, "Time is the scarcest resource and, unless it is managed, nothing else can be managed." In fact, American businesses believe so deeply in the concept of time management that they spend billions of dollars each year sending their employees to workshops and seminars on the subject.

The many books written on time management could fill an entire wing at your local library. However, the concept of time management is not nearly that complicated. It's actually quite simple when you realize that you are not trying to manage time, but rather the events of your day.

MANAGE EVENTS – NOT TIME

You can't manage time. You can't save it. You can't roll it back. Time simply marches on, completely unaffected by how you attempt to "manage" it. However, you can manage the events in your life. Therefore, although you can't affect how quickly or slowly the next year goes by (trust me – it will seem much quicker than you'd like), you can affect the events you experience in this next year.

When you look at time management from this perspective, it's not so complicated. For instance, let's suppose someone informs you that at exactly 11:00 a.m. tomorrow, an unmarked bag containing $1 million will be left in front of the post office for the first person who finds it. Could you "manage" to be in front of the post office at precisely 11:00 a.m. tomorrow? Of course, you could. In fact, I bet you'd get there a few minutes ahead of time!

But wait! I've just remembered. You have a dentist appointment tomorrow at 10:30 a.m. Well, you certainly can't miss your dental appointment. After all, your spouse has been bugging you for weeks to go to the dentist. It's been at least a year since you've had a cleaning. Well, you could always try to hurry your dentist through your appointment and hope that by the time you get to the post office, the bag is still there. Sound like a good plan?

Not really, right? In fact, it sounds a little crazy. Who in their right mind would possibly miss out on the chance to receive $1 million for the sake of a dental appointment? You're not going to believe me when I tell you this, but you make this kind of decision at least twice a week.

The consequences are never outlined as clearly, but the decision-making process is the same. Perhaps you missed a big sale because you were dealing with a customer service issue while a competitor was calling on "your" prospect. Or perhaps you were too busy to attend your child's basketball games because you were working overtime for a company that eventually laid you off.

154

Or how many times have you gone into work to accomplish an important task and ended up accomplishing everything but that task? I've done this dozens of times. I'd arrive to work earlier than usual and get right to work. However, soon the phone would ring and I'd need to make a quick call to the vendor in Cleveland and another call to an important client in Philadelphia. Then, of course, I had to sit in on a product launch meeting at 10 a.m., which invariably ran late. This left me scrambling to make it to my 11 a.m. meeting with the new HR director. And you can guess how the rest of the day went. Before long, it was 7 p.m. and I'd spent my entire day working on everyone's priorities but my own. And I was the "boss."

If you talk to corporate executives all over the country, this is not an uncommon experience, nor is it a new problem. In fact, the legendary Charles Schwab had this same problem in the 1930s. He hired a business consultant named Ivy Lee to help him better "manage" his time. Reportedly, Schwab told Lee, "Show me a way to get more things done, and I'll pay you anything within reason."

Lee gave Schwab a blank sheet of paper and instructed him to write down the most important tasks he had to perform the next day. Lee then told Schwab to number them in order of importance. Lee then said, "When you arrive in the morning, begin at number one on the list and stay with it until you complete it. Then begin number two and continue through the list all day long – only working on your most important task. If at the end of the day you haven't completed your entire list, then don't worry. You couldn't have completed everything with any other method but at least, you will have accomplished the most important tasks. Make this your habit every working day, and then send me a check for what you think it's worth."

To his credit, Schwab followed this rather simplistic advice, and within a few weeks, he sent Lee a check for $25,000.

Schwab said that the $25,000 was his most valuable invest-
ment and credited working off a list as the idea that turned
Bethlehem Steel into the largest independent steel producer
at that time.

Now, I'll admit that this system of event management
may not work for everyone. After all, unless you are your
own boss, you will have to rearrange your priorities to fit the
demands of others. And even then it isn't always possible to
work on the most important task. For instance, let's suppose
you live in New York and your first priority for the day is to
contact a prospective client on the West coast. In that case,
you may not be able to reach that person until the afternoon, so it doesn't make much sense to sit around waiting
until that person arrives in the office.

Nevertheless, there is some wisdom to this system. As a
general rule, you should spend your time working on the
most important task you can work on *at that moment*. Of
course, this assumes that you know which task is most important. In fact, it further assumes you have a list of tasks to
prioritize.

A key element to event management is to list the events
of your day. Before you go to bed each night, you should
make a list of all your appointments and all the things you
want to accomplish the next day. From this list, you should
prioritize and work from there, starting with the most important task on the list.

Now, the reason I suggest you make your list the night
before is to give your subconscious mind a head-start on the
tasks. After all, it's going to be up all night anyway. It might
as well be doing something useful.

Seriously, I have had some of my most brilliant ideas
while I was sleeping. In fact, we all have. How many times
have you awakened in the morning only to have the solution
to a problem "magically" at your fingertips? Well, it wasn't
magic. It was your subconscious mind working overtime.

However, your subconscious mind can't perform tasks from a list you don't make.

Jump the Gun

As the sprinters line up at the starting line of a race, the starter yells, "On your mark, get set, go!" As you get ready to start the next leg of your DASH, I want to give the same instructions to you.

On Your Mark—Now is the time to find your mark: the place you are going to stand and, more importantly, what you are going to stand *for*. What do you want to achieve next year? Is this going to be the year you finally quit smoking, learn French, start your own business, mend a broken relationship with a loved one, get out of debt, or lose sixty pounds? If so, now is the time to make your decision and take a stand.

Get Set—If you've ever been to a track meet, then you know that sprinters don't just show up at the track, walk to the starting line, and start running. They first spend some time warming up before the race. They wouldn't consider starting the race without first stretching and running back and forth down the track.

You need some time to warm up as well. You need to spend some time stretching; enlarging your skills, your knowledge, your financial resources, and your network of associates. You also need to make a few "dry runs" before the real race starts in January. For instance, if your dream is to be the next American Idol, warm up by singing in a local karaoke bar. Or if your dream is to become a world-renowned fashion designer, warm up by designing holiday outfits for your nieces and nephews.

Go!—In the Olympic 100-meter dash, the sprinters can only start running when the starter fires his pistol. However, in your DASH, you're allowed to cheat a little bit. There is no need for you to wait until 12:00 a.m. on New Year's Day to start on your goal of losing sixty pounds next year. You can jump the gun by starting today. Why not lose ten pounds during the next two months so that you are already in full stride when the race officially begins?

In fact, some goals can be accomplished only by jumping the gun. For instance, let's suppose that you are a salesperson, and you've set a goal to double your sales this year. The only way to accomplish that goal is to jump the gun and start setting up your January appointments now. The same principle applies to almost any goal. Remember, a good January starts in November.

And, by all means, if you must wait until January to get started on your goal, don't do anything in the next two months to make your goal more difficult to achieve. For instance, if you decide that next year is the year when you finally payoff your credit cards, don't make it harder by charging them to the limit this holiday season. The same thing applies to weight loss. It will be difficult enough to lose any excess weight you may be carrying now. Don't make it even harder by putting on an extra fifteen pounds during the holidays.

Therefore, as your starter for this year's leg of your DASH, let me just say, "On your mark, get set, jump the gun!"

THOUGHTS FOR YOUR DASH

Determination
> "Obstacles cannot crush me. Every obstacle yields to stern resolve. He who is fixed to a star does not change his mind."
>
> LEONARDO DA VINCI

Attitude
> "A positive attitude may not solve all your problems, but it will annoy enough people to make it worth the effort."
>
> HERM ALBRIGHT

Success
> "Try not to become a man of success but rather to become a man of value."
>
> ALBERT EINSTEIN

Happiness
> "Most folks are about as happy as they make up their minds to be."
>
> ABRAHAM LINCOLN

CHAPTER 15

No Man is an Island

No matter what your mission in life, know that it will require the assistance and cooperation of other people. The simple truth is that no one person possesses enough skills, talents and energy to accomplish anything of significance. The great individual leaders of our time were all surrounded by an army of people who made it possible for them to achieve goals.

Take Dr. Martin Luther King, Jr., who won the Nobel Peace Prize in 1964 for his work as a civil rights leader. This is a remarkable individual achievement, yet it required *massive* cooperation with others. In city after city throughout the South, thousands of men and women took to the streets in nonviolent protest. Now, can you imagine if Dr. King had tried to stage a march all by himself? He would have been considered just a lone nut and probably jailed in obscurity. Instead, by drawing thousands of people to his cause, he was literally able to change the course of history.

The same thing could be said of Mary Kay Ash, founder of Mary Kay Cosmetics. She had a dream of creating a major cosmetics company, but she would have had a difficult time turning this dream into a reality if she attempted to distribute products by herself. Instead, she set up a multilevel marketing company, in which thousands of other women sell the products and recruit others to help. As of this writing, Mary Kay Inc. has more than 800,000 sales consultants in 37 countries that generate sales of more than $1 billion each year. Obviously the phenomenal success of this company is not simply the result of the efforts of one extraordinary woman.

Henry Ford is another classic example. During his time, he was one of the richest men in America. He became wealthy by creating a company that was on the cutting edge of a relatively new technology – automotive travel – despite the fact that Henry Ford only had a sixth grade education. However, Ford understood the importance of working with other people. In fact, he often explained his success by saying, "I am not the smartest, but I surround myself with competent people."

BE A "PEOPLE PERSON"

If you are going to accomplish your mission, you will need to do the same thing. However, this won't be difficult if you remember one thing – people hire, promote, befriend and give money to people they *like*.

Encourage Others

One way to be liked is to treat people how you would like to be treated. In other words, live by the "Golden Rule." Each of us has a basic need to be liked. In fact, in most cases, people like us not for who we are, but for how we make them feel about themselves. And, after the basic needs of food and shelter, perhaps our greatest need is to feel appreciated.

Unfortunately, this need isn't always fulfilled. The renowned speaker Cavett Roberts once said:

"Three billion people on the face of the earth go to bed hungry every night, but four billion people go to bed hungry for a simple word of encouragement and recognition."

If you want people to be drawn to you, find a way to fulfill this need. Any time you have an opportunity to extend sincere praise, take it. Of course, the key word is that your praise must be *sincere*. People can see through phony praise and will either think you are being dishonest, or worse, sarcastic.

Fortunately, it's never necessary to give false praise because the opportunities for sincere praise are boundless. Let's say suppose you work in an office with someone. In this case, chances are excellent that, at least once a day, this person will do something worthy of praise. Remember, you don't need to throw a ticker-tape parade – simply saying "Great job" will usually suffice.

Now, you may be thinking, "That's easy for him to say. He doesn't work with my assistant." Well, please know that praise and encouragement are even more important for the problem employee. And this applies to the problem child, problem neighbor and problem spouse as well. If someone has let you down, try pulling them aside and saying something like, "Although your performance in this last matter has been disappointing, I know that you are a better [employee/friend/family member] than that. I just wanted to let you know that I still have every confidence in you and am looking forward to your future performance."

How do you think someone would respond to a statement like this? How would you respond to this statement? Wouldn't you try harder next time? I know that I would. The bottom line is that people generally live up to the level of expectations placed upon them.

Give the Benefit of the Doubt

Another part of living by the Golden Rule is to give people the benefit of the doubt. A classic story about this involves a man who boarded a subway train with his five young children. The man immediately found a seat while the children began wreaking havoc – shouting, running, climbing and jumping all over the train. Several irritated passengers looked at the father to restore order, but he just sat there on the bench with his eyes closed, seemingly oblivious to the commotion his children were causing. Finally, one woman reached her limit and walked over to the man, tapped him on the shoulder and said, "Sir! You really should do something about your kids. They are disturbing everyone on the train."

The father just looked at the woman in a dazed manner and then, finally appearing to realize the situation, said "Oh yeah. I guess you're right. It's just that we just came back from their mother's funeral, and I'm not sure what to say to them."

Can you imagine how bad the stranger must have felt at that moment? Wouldn't it have been better had she given the man the benefit of the doubt by assuming that he was ordinarily a good parent and that there must be some extenuating circumstance to explain his lack of responsiveness? In that case, she could have approached the man by saying something like, "I see that you are having a hard time with the kids today. Is there anything that I can do to help?"

This is a great way to handle disappointments with the people in your life. If someone misses an important appointment, don't assume they simply blew it off. Instead, give them the benefit of the doubt. Work from the assumption that they would not have missed the meeting unless something much more pressing came up. In that way, if it turns out that they were injured in a car accident on the way to the meeting or one of their children became ill the night before, you won't feel like the woman on the subway. Most importantly, you'll gain an ally.

Tune in to WII-FM

Perhaps the quickest and best way to gain allies is to clearly demonstrate that it's in their best interest to promote yours. The reality is that most of our antennas are tuned in to *WII-FM* ("What's In It For Me"). We all have personal objectives that we are trying to reach. The key to getting others to support your cause is to show how supporting you will bring them closer to their own objectives.

> **"We are interested in others when they are interested in us."**
> **—Publilius Syrus**

When I began my career on Wall Street, I learned quickly that I could get people to part with thousands, even millions of dollars if I could demonstrate that it was in their best interest to do so. In fact, to my knowledge, not one of my clients ever entered into a relationship with me for *my* benefit. They became clients to make more money. The fact that I also benefited from the relationship was merely coincidental.

And the same principle applies whether your mission is starting a for-profit business or a non-profit social organization. People will give their time, their money and other resources if you can demonstrate that it's in their best interest to do so. Remember, it's in everyone's best interest to eliminate cancer, teen pregnancy or homelessness. The key is to simply find the other person's "hot buttons" and demonstrate that your mission is aligned with those interests.

For instance, in one of Aesop's fables, a peasant becomes disturbed that his apple tree bears no fruit. He grabs an axe and starts to cut down the tree when the sparrows and grasshoppers plead with the peasant not to cut down their home.

165

The peasant paid no attention to their requests and continued chopping away at the tree until he reached its hollow. There he found a hive full of honey. Upon tasting the sweetness of the honeycomb the peasant threw down his axe and regarded the tree as sacred.

As you can see, the peasant wasn't concerned about the plight of the sparrows or the grasshoppers. He decided to allow the tree to stand because it suited his own purpose – it housed the honeycomb. In some cases, you will be like the sparrows and the grasshoppers. During those times, make sure you point out the honeycombs to the person with the power to cut down your tree.

Practice Doing the Little Things

In many cases, the difference between success and failure is miniscule. For instance, in many Olympic events, one-tenth of a second can mean the difference between a gold medal and no medal. The same is true when dealing with people. Often, the only reason that one person gets the job or the contract or the date and another person doesn't is because of some seemingly insignificant courtesy. So I urge you to "practice" doing the little things that count.

Please and Thank You. These really are the magic words when dealing with people. They are much more powerful than "voila" or "alakazam" in opening the vaults of love and true friendship. Send thank you notes, make thank you calls and even send flowers and small gifts when appropriate.

Remember the Name of Everyone You Meet. It has been said that the most beautiful word in the English dictionary for each of us is our own name. And this applies not only to "important" people, but also to their colleagues, assistants and family members. People will be extremely impressed that you went to the trouble to remember their names. And by all means, don't just rely on your memory. Keep a record of your daily contacts. Whenever you are going to visit a client or friend, take a moment to review the list of that person's colleagues and associates so you can dazzle them with your fantastic "memory."

Accept "No's" Like a Professional. When someone refuses to buy your product, lend you money or otherwise support your dream, do not become bitter. And by all means, don't use harsh words that may end the relationship. Remember, if someone says "No," they are only saying "No" to you *today*. In time, things may change. Later, your idea may seem workable after all, or you may want to approach the person with a completely different idea. But neither will be possible if you react hastily to the first "No" and permanently damage the relationship.

Correct Negative Thinking and Actions. People have an amazing ability to pick up on negative thoughts. If you are presenting a proposal that you don't believe in, the listener will be able to tell. This is partly because 93 percent of our communication is nonverbal. People pick up on facial expressions and body language better than language alone. Therefore, you must be completely honest with yourself and make sure that you really believe in your ideas before presenting them to others.

Take Responsibility for Setbacks. There are few things more distasteful than witnessing someone trying to blame others for their shortcomings. There may be 40,000 reasons for failure, but not a single *excuse*. Therefore, make sure that, when you fail to meet someone's expectations — and you will — that you accept responsibility and take it upon yourself to rectify the situation.

Include Everyone in Your Efforts. We often miss obvious opportunities to enlist the help of others because we become blinded by our "favorites." We make a list of the people that we just *know* are going to be excited by our cause and neglect to ask others, only to learn later that these people aren't nearly as interested as we thought. The solution is to give everyone the opportunity to become involved in your mission. If it's truly a worthwhile mission, then it's only right to share the joy.

Consistently Contact and Re-contact. Always keep in mind that most sales are only closed after the fifth contact. Unfortunately, 48 percent of salespeople only make one contact, 25 percent make two contacts, 15 percent contact three times, and only 12 percent call back more than three times. But this 12 percent gets 88 percent of the business. Even if you are not in the business of selling a product or service, you are in the business of selling ideas – you sell yourself on the idea to go to work or to buy a new car, you sell your children on the idea of getting good grades and staying out of the trouble – the list goes on and on.

Enthusiasm. Genuine enthusiasm for your mission will do more to draw people to you than anything else. In fact, you could have all of the reason in the world on your side, but if it's not backed by enthusiasm, you are going to have a difficult time winning people to your cause.

Avoid Gossip

Finally, if you want to endear yourself to others, make sure that you avoid gossip. I will confess that this isn't always easy because it's fun to be the messenger at times. However, before spreading any bad news about another person, remember to ask: "Is it true? Is it fair? Is it necessary?" If the answer to any of these questions is "no" (and it usually is), then keep quiet.

Gossip can be devastating to its subject and it can be equally devastating to the messenger. Think about it. You probably know someone who continually spreads gossip. Do you like this person? More importantly, do you trust this person? If you had a problem, would you seek out their advice? Of course not. And that's the way people feel when you spread gossip and rumors. After hearing your tale of gossip, they may be unsure about whether or not to believe it, but they know that you are not to be trusted.

My Name Is Gossip
Author Unknown

I have no respect for justice.
I maim without killing. I break hearts and ruin lives.
I am cunning, malicious, and gather strength with age.
The more I am quoted the more I am believed.
I flourish at every level of society.
My victims are helpless.
They cannot protect themselves against me, because
I have no name and no face.
To track me down is impossible. The harder you try the
    more elusive I become.
I am nobody's friend.
Once I tarnish a reputation, it is never the same.
I topple governments and wreck marriages.
I ruin careers and cause sleepless nights, heartaches,
    and indigestion.
I spawn suspicion and generate grief.
I make headlines and headaches.
Remember, before you repeat a story, ask yourself:
Is it true? Is it fair? Is it necessary?
If not, do not repeat it.
KEEP QUIET!

There is No "I" in DASH

As you may be aware, last week, I had the extreme privilege and honor to announce that Mike Jarvis, one of the premier college basketball coaches in the country, had joined the DASH team as a life coach. In the days since making this announcement, our offices have been flooded with calls from the media and clients looking to be coached by one of the best coaches anywhere.

As I've had some time to reflect on the excitement that this partnership has caused, it has made me realize just how important teamwork is in life. Of course, in the sporting world, the importance of teamwork is readily apparent. For instance, in the game of basketball, one player, no matter how great, is not enough to make a winning team.

This point was illustrated very well in the career of the late Wilt Chamberlain. Quite simply, Wilt Chamberlain was the most dominating player in the history of the NBA. To this day, his name appears in the record books more than seventy times. His scoring feats are legendary and may never be surpassed. On March 2, 1962, he scored 100 points in a single game. That year, he scored more than 70 points in three other games and ended the season averaging more than 50 points per game. The man was simply a scoring machine. In seven of his first eight years in league, he led the NBA in scoring, and he also led the league in rebounding in six of those years.

Nevertheless, despite all of his personal success, Chamberlain's teams did not win a single NBA championship during this time. However, all of that changed during the 1967–1968 season when Chamberlain's Philadelphia Warriors won the title. As you might guess,

Chamberlain's stats were once again stellar that year, but not in the way you would imagine. Wilt did not lead the league in scoring that year. In fact, he was far from the league leader in scoring. That year, he averaged just 24.3 points per game, which was 13 points lower than his career season average up to that point.

However, he did lead the league in one important category—assists. Although Chamberlain's career average had been fewer than four assists per game in his first eight seasons in the NBA, he averaged 8.6 assists per game during the championship year. Of course, this was not a coincidence. When Chamberlain turned his attention from his personal scoring records to helping his teammates score, he became a champion.

The same thing happens in the game of life as well. None of us is talented, smart, or skilled enough to make it on our own. The only way we will ever achieve any significant victory is by getting others involved and *assisting* them in putting a few points on the board with us.

I really believe that this has been the key to my success in life—my ability to "pass the ball." When I ran my brokerage firm, I didn't try to do everything myself; that would have been suicide! Instead, I found hard-working and talented people to work alongside me, and *together*, we turned our brokerage firm into a multimillion dollar company. One of my proudest accomplishments is that in just a few years, I helped more than thirty people realize their dreams of becoming a millionaire. And in the process, I didn't do too poorly either.

How are your assist stats this year? Are you trying to carry the load all by yourself or are you passing off (delegating) assignments to others?

I understand that this can be a difficult thing to do, particularly if you are already a skilled and accomplished person. There is a tendency to think that no one can do the job as well as you can. And this may well be true, but it is no less reason to delegate anyway. Think about Wilt Chamberlain. He was the greatest scorer of all-time. No one could put the ball in the basket more consistently than he could, yet he realized that he could never win if he was doing all the scoring. If he wanted to achieve the ultimate success in basketball (an NBA championship), he was going to have to let others do some of the scoring for him.

If you want the ultimate prize in life (whatever that is for you), you are going to have to do the same thing. For instance, if you want your company's business to increase, you must delegate increasing responsibility to your managers and employees. Or if you are a salesperson and you want your sales to increase, you must delegate increasing responsibility to your support staff and other company personnel. Remember, the more you let others shine, the more it reflects on you.

"Alone we can do so little; together we can do so much."

Helen Keller

THOUGHTS FOR YOUR DASH

Determination
> "When building a team, I always search first for people who love to win. If I can't find any of those, I look for people who hate to lose."
>
> H. ROSS PEROT

Attitude
> "What happens to a man is less significant than what happens within him."
>
> LOUIS L. MANN

Success
> "The person who tries to live alone will not succeed as a human being. His heart withers if it does not answer another heart. His mind shrinks away if he hears only the echoes of his own thoughts and finds no other inspiration."
>
> PEARL S. BUCK

Happiness
> "Now and then it's good to pause in our pursuit of happiness and just be happy."
>
> GUILLAUME APOLLINAIRE

CHAPTER 16

Get a Helping Hand

In your mission to make your dash meaningful, you're going to need a lot of help from others. And there are certain people you should be cultivating specifically, and these are *mentors*. Mentoring has long been recognized by successful people as critical to success. You simply don't have enough time to make all of the mistakes yourself, so why not learn from someone who has already been down the path you want to travel? You can literally take decades off the length of your journey by heeding the advice of others who have made it. They can show you the potholes and detours – and even provide you with shortcuts.

For instance, let's suppose you are trying to bake a chocolate cake. If you know this recipe, then this is a simple task. However, if you don't know the recipe, you are going to have to get extremely lucky to bake anything that resembles a chocolate cake. For one, you need to know what ingredients go into a chocolate cake. Obviously, if you bake your cake without eggs or milk, you are going to end up with a unique cake, to say the least. You also need to know the right order of the ingredients. For instance, if you mix the icing into the batter and bake it with the rest of the cake, you are going to have a problem. In short, without a recipe, your chances of baking a delicious chocolate cake are slim. As a result, only the most foolhardy person would even try.

But many people happily start new business ventures without a recipe. In fairness, they have a general idea of the ingredients of success. They obtain a degree or a certificate. They buy a new computer or other special equipment. They have business cards and stationary printed. And then they go about the process of trial and error to determine the proper recipe.

But wouldn't it be so much easier (not to mention cheaper) to find someone who already has the recipe? After all, there is probably someone already doing what you want to do. Wouldn't it be smarter to get the recipe from them, rather than learning the hard way?

IT'S A WIN-WIN SITUATION

The really interesting thing is that successful people are usually more than willing to help you. First of all, many of these people had mentors themselves and are only too happy to "return the favor." Second, successful people understand that the best way to learn something is to teach it to someone else. Having someone to mentor gives them another opportunity to fully digest the lessons they've learned and put them into practice in their own lives. And having someone that looks up to them forces mentors to practice what they preach. In fact, this is one of the most valuable aspects of coaching for me. As I work with my clients to help them overcome negative self-talk or procrastination, I am forced to watch my own behavior in those areas. After all, it's not enough for me to merely give the message; I must also *be* the message.

> **"The way to be successful is to follow the advice you give to others."**
> **—Unknown**

176

DEMYSTIFYING SUCCESS

Another advantage of developing a relationship with a mentor is that you can begin to see successful people for who they are – ordinary people who consistently take ordinary actions to achieve extraordinary results. When I was broke, I thought of the wealthy as almost mythical creatures with magical powers. However, the more I came to know them, the more I began to see them as regular people who struggle with the same issues as the rest of us.

In a sense, developing a personal relationship with a successful person allows you to go behind the curtain and unmask the Great Oz. Remember in *The Wizard of Oz* when Dorothy and the gang first went to see the wizard. They were in awe (and even frightened) of his great "power." However, once the curtain was drawn back, they found themselves face-to-face with an ordinary man.

Getting behind the curtain is important to us for another reason. It allows us to learn that, in most cases, success is 1 percent inspiration and 99 percent perspiration. This becomes quite evident from close-up, but impossible to see from far away.

In one sense, it's like watching the Kentucky Derby. From the grandstands, the horses seem to glide effortlessly along at tremendous speeds. However, the jockey has a much different perspective. He hears the labored and painful breathing or the horse, the hot air steaming from its nostrils, and feels the sweat pouring from the animal. The jockey understands that a race horse struggles while making it look easy.

Hopefully, this knowledge will give you comfort as you make your own dash through life. You will know that your struggles are not unique and that success is not easy for anyone, even those who make it look effortless. As Robert Collier once said, "The great are great to us only because we are on our knees. Let us arise!"

BE A MENTOR

Also, please know that it's never too early for you to act as a mentor to someone else. Regardless of how far you may be from your goal, you are much closer than other people. As you dash through life, make sure you reach out a helping hand to someone who may have just fallen at the last hurdle. You can do this by simply sharing an encouraging word. You would be surprised by the power of a kind word.

In fact, much of my success can be indirectly traced to the kind words of my Fairy Godfather. A complete stranger was able to completely change the direction of my life by believing in me at a time when I didn't even believe in myself. And there is a benefit in this for you, too. You get to hear the message again.

If you hear a positive message, then you receive the benefit of that message just once. However, if you share it with ten other people, you get the benefit of that message ten times. In the end, you get much more power from sharing. Kind words are like perfume. You can't sprinkle them on others without getting a little bit on yourself.

In Order to G-E-T You Must A-S-K

Last week, I had the privilege of speaking to a group of students at Hofstra University. After the talk, I took questions from the students. Amazingly, although my talk was only forty-five minutes long, the question and answer session lasted over ninety minutes. I fielded question after question. These students were earnestly seeking the answers to the success in every area of life—career, finances, health, relationships, you name it. Three of the students even offered to treat me to a round of golf so that they could have an opportunity to ask even more questions.

And although the experience was certainly exhausting, it was also exhilarating. Although they may not realize it now, these students are closer to success than they think because they are learning perhaps the most important life skill—the ability to ask.

Much of my success in life has come from asking the right questions of the right people. When I went into the brokerage business, I asked for the advice of successful brokers. When I went into this business, I asked for the advice of successful coaches and speakers. I simply didn't have the time or the energy to make all the mistakes that could be avoided by heeding the advice of those who had already been where I wanted to go. As Minna Antrim wrote in her classic work, Naked Truth and Veiled Allusions, "Experience is a great teacher but she sends in terrific bills."

How much is experience costing you in terms of your finances, your business, or your family life? If there is an area in your life that you'd like to improve upon (and we all have at least one of those areas), then perhaps it's time to seek the advice of wise counsel. Why take ten or twenty years to stumble upon the key to a healthy marriage, spiritual enlightenment, or your dream job when a trusted mentor can walk you right into the promised land?

I believe that one thing that keeps us from seeking advice is stubborn pride. We don't want to admit to others (or even ourselves) that we don't know what we're doing. However, in our attempt to hide our ignorance, we only prolong it. According to a famous Chinese proverb, "Those who ask questions may be fools for five minutes, but those who do not are fools forever." Therefore, the next time you're in a position to ask questions of someone who has already achieved what you want to achieve, do it. Swallow your pride; it's not fattening.

Of course, just as important as it is to ask the questions, it's equally important to ask them to the right people. Often, we seek advice from anyone who is handy at the moment. We ask our friends, our families, or the customer next to us in the checkout lane at the supermarket. We ask anyone but the person who has actually done what we are trying to do. Remember, the fool asks the wise man for advice, while the wise man asked the experienced.

Therefore, although your best friend may have an IQ of 180, she may not be the person to ask about starting a dry cleaning business. The person to ask in this case is the man or woman who owns seven dry cleaning establishments and is in the process of opening number eight. This person will *know* the answers that your genius friend can only hope to arrive at through mere brainpower.

In some cases, this presents a challenge because we don't always know people with this kind of experience. However, this shouldn't stop us. Where there is a will there is a way. And one of these ways is to simply seek out the top performers in your chosen field. This is exactly what I did in building my current company, DASH Systems, LLC.

When I first got into the motivation business, I sought out the help of one of the big names in the business. I simply approached the man and let him know that I admired his work and wanted to make the same kind of contribution to the world. Not only was he good enough to offer advice but he invited me out to San Diego to meet some of the legends in the field of personal development.

And why was I able to get such wonderful advice? Because I asked for it. It's really that simple. Successful people are usually more than happy to help others. After all, that's how most of us "made it" in the first place, by getting help from others. We are more than happy to return the favor, but you have to take the first step. Therefore, seek out the leaders in your field and boldly ask for their help. I think you will be pleasantly surprised by the results.

"You don't always get what you ask for, but you never get what you don't ask for...unless it's contagious!"
Franklyn Broude

THOUGHTS FOR YOUR DASH

Determination
> "The battle is all over except the 'shouting' when one knows what is wanted and has made up his mind to get it, whatever the price may be."
> NAPOLEON HILL

Attitude
> "One man has enthusiasm for thirty minutes, another for thirty days, but it is the man who has it for thirty years who makes a success of his life."
> EDWARD B. BUTLER

Success
> "When you stop learning, stop listening, stop looking and asking questions, always new questions, then it is time to die."
> LILLIAN SMITH

Happiness
> "Wisdom is the supreme part of happiness."
> SOPHOCLES

CHAPTER 17

Walk Away From Your Past

As much as I encourage you to seek out and find mentors, I also encourage you to avoid certain people and activities. This is particularly true if those people and activities are part of a lifestyle that you are trying to leave behind. For instance, if you have had a problem with alcohol in the past, then you'll obviously want to stay out of bars. However, you may also need to stay away from your old drinking buddies, even in non-drinking situations.

There's a story about a gentleman who was walking down a residential street when he noticed a man struggling with a washing machine at the doorway of his house. The gentleman volunteered to help and the two men began to work and struggle with the bulky appliance. After several minutes of fruitless effort, the gentleman said to the homeowner: "We'll never get this washing machine in there!" And the homeowner replied: "In? I'm trying to move it *out*!" The point is that you won't get very far in your dash if you team with people who are moving in the opposite direction.

LEAVE THE HERD

In prison, I met a number of people who truly were victims of "hanging with the wrong crowd." They weren't bad people, simply people who had chosen bad relationships. They accompanied a "friend" on a joy ride and ended up in prison for grand theft auto. Or they stored a box for a "friend," only to learn during a police raid that the box contained drugs or weapons. Now, don't get me wrong, I'm not saying that these people were innocent, but they certainly allowed their "friendships" to get them into a lot more trouble than they would have chosen for themselves.

"Every man becomes, to a certain extent, what the people he generally converses with are."
—Philip Dormer Stanhope

The simple truth is that those who hang with dogs get fleas. Regardless of what we'd all like to believe, we are heavily influenced by those around us. This principle is wonderfully illustrated in Leonardo Da Vinci's story of "The Nut and the Bell Tower":

A nut found itself carried by a crow to the top of a tall bell tower. However, the crow soon dropped the nut and it fell into a crevice in the walls of the bell tower. The nut then appealed to the bell tower for protection. The wall, moved with compassion, was content to shelter the nut in the spot where it had fallen.

Within a short time, the nut burst open. Its roots reached in between the crevices of the stones and began to push them apart; its shoots pressed up toward the sky. They soon rose above the building and, as the twisted roots grew thicker, they began to thrust the walls apart and force the ancient stones from their old places. Then the wall, too late and in vain, cried the cause of its destruction, and in short time it fell in ruin.

Sadly, this is what happens to us when we let the negative influences of others into our hearts and minds. At first, these influences are simply tiny acorns, which slip into the crevices (or cracks) in our character. But soon these influences sprout branches and begin to push into other areas of our lives. Before we know it, they overrun us.

YOU CAN'T GO HOME AGAIN

When we make a dramatic change in our lives, we are so excited that we want to share it with others, particularly those who are still suffering through the problems we recently overcame. This is a noble intention, but it's a strategy fraught with peril.

For one, people only change when they truly *want* to change. We sometimes think that everyone would want to change if they just knew what we did, but that is simply not true.

Think about it. How many of us honestly believe that cheeseburgers, french fries, chocolate shakes and cigarettes are the four basic food groups? We all *know* that these things are bad for us, but it doesn't stop us from consuming them daily. Knowledge alone is not enough. There must be a genuine desire on the part of the other person to change. Moreover, even if it's possible that someone can have a positive effect on your old friends, *you* are not that person. The sad truth is that people who knew you "way back when" are the least able to see the changes you've made.

For example, let's suppose that for most of your life, you've been an unreliable person but you've recently committed to changing your ways. If you meet a new friend, they have no knowledge of your past and will likely give you the benefit of the doubt. As we discussed earlier, people generally live up to the expectations of others. As you result, you have a better chance of being reliable in a relationship with someone new.

However, this isn't the case with an old friend. With good reason, it's going to be difficult to convince them you've changed. After all, you have a longer history of being unreliable, and one or two positive experiences will not erase 20 or 30 years of bad ones.

So what's the answer? It's simple: You want to be around people who will support you and serve as a good example for your new way of being. It would be nice if those people were your old friends but the truth is that you can't change the people in your life – so change the *people* in your life.

I realize this may seem harsh, but it may be necessary for you to grow. Remember, we all assume many roles during the course of our day (e.g., worker, parent, spouse, neighbor, etc.). Regardless of the number of roles, at the end of the day, you are only one person. You simply cannot live two separate lives in one body. You have to make a choice as to the type of life you will live and then move towards that lifestyle wholeheartedly. And part of that process is leaving behind those activities and people that are not in harmony with the new you.

Take a Load Off

There is an ancient story of two men who were walking along when they came across an old woman stopped at a stream. When the men asked why the woman was just standing on the bank of the stream, she explained that she was afraid to walk across because, in her frail condition, she could slip and the currents could sweep her away. Sympathetic to her plight, the two men lifted the woman, carried her across the stream, and continued on their way.

A little while later, one of the men said, "I can't believe we agreed to carry that woman across the stream. Now, my back is killing me!" His companion walked along in silence.

However, it wasn't long before the first man began complaining again. "Why did we do such a foolish thing? I'm going to be sore for days!" Once again, his companion walked on in silence. Noticing that the other man was walking without pain, the first man stopped and asked his friend, "Why doesn't your back hurt?" Without breaking stride, the man answered, "Because I put the old woman down several miles ago."

Therefore, my question to you is this. Are you still caring around something that you should have dropped long ago? Perhaps, you've been hurt by a harsh comment from a supposed friend or loved one and you're still carrying around the pain of rejection, ridicule, or betrayal. Or perhaps, you experienced failure in a business venture or a relationship and you're still carrying around the feelings of inadequacy, disappointment, or shame. In any event, don't you think now would be a good time to unburden yourself of that load?

As you DASH toward your goals, now would be a good time to shed some of that excess baggage. After all, do you really need it? Do you need to constantly relive stinging words of criticism? Do you really need to relive a betrayal of trust? I don't think so.

Amazingly, many people carry around resentment and anger under the false impression that it will fuel their drive toward success. They think to themselves, "I'm going to show them!" Well, if this is your attitude, I have some pretty bad news for you: "No, you won't!" Your former tormentors don't care. In all likelihood, they never cared, but they certainly aren't sitting around five, ten, or even fifty years later thinking, "Hey, I wonder how Joe is doing. I hope he didn't ultimately succeed. That would ruin my day."

Therefore, if you think that your success is going to somehow "even the score," you're going to be disappointed. For example, the guidance counselor who voted me "Most Likely Not to Succeed" isn't crying in her Cheerios each morning because I managed to defy her prediction for my future. Therefore, if I had made the sole purpose of my success to "show her," I would have fulfilled her prophesy because I am unlikely to ever succeed in changing her attitude about me.

Besides, as the old saying goes, "What she thinks of me is none of my business." In the same way, what your former boss, former lover, or ex-friend thinks of you is none of your business. What really matters is what you think about you. And although you can choose to focus on getting even, I'd rather get ahead. Therefore, instead of spending your time and energy on changing the perception of someone who may be blind to your true value, just dump that emotional baggage and run your race. The results will speak for themselves.

"A chip on the shoulder is too heavy a piece of baggage to carry through life."

John Hancock

THOUGHTS FOR YOUR DASH

Determination
> For better or worse, our future will be determined in large part by our dreams and by the struggle to make them real."
>
> MIHALY CSIKSZENTMIHALYI

Attitude
> "Bad things do happen; how I respond to them defines my character and the quality of my life."
>
> WALTER JOHNSON

Success
> "You may have to fight a battle more than once to win."
>
> MARGARET THATCHER

Happiness
> "Depression is nourished by a lifetime of ungrieved and unforgiven hurts."
>
> PENELOPE SWEET

CHAPTER 18

Get Friendly With Failure

For much of this book, I've relentlessly pushed the concept of positive thinking. But the fact is that YOU WILL FAIL. You will fail in school. You will fail in business. You will fail in relationships. At best, your dash will be filled with a series of failures. As Dr. Robert Anthony says, "If at first you don't succeed, you're about average!"

This may sound terribly negative, but it's not meant that way. The simple truth is that failure is a part of life and an even bigger part of success. The great winners in life are usually those who have experienced the most defeats. Consider the record of this "loser":

He failed in business at age 22. He was defeated in an election for the state legislature at age 23. He failed again in business the next year. At age 27, he suffered a nervous breakdown. Over the next four years, he was defeated in races for speaker and elector. At age 34, he was defeated in a race for Congress. At age 46, he was defeated in a Senate race. The next year, he ran for Vice President and lost. Two years later, he ran for the Senate and lost again. At age 51, he was elected as the 16th President of the United States. Of course, the man to whom I'm referring is Abraham Lincoln.

I don't think there are many people who would consider Abraham Lincoln to be a loser. I'm certainly not one of them. This man is arguably the greatest figure of the 19ᵗʰ century, yet his life was filled with setbacks. His story shows that you don't need to succeed very often to be a "winner" in life. However, what you need to do is to keep going in spite of failure.

NEVER GIVE UP

Thomas Edison created the incandescent light bulb after 10,000 unsuccessful attempts. Edison tried using all kinds of materials to serve as a filament for his light bulb. Each time he produced a fiber that didn't conduct electricity, he tossed it out the window. In a year, those fibers reached the second story of his home. In fact, even when he discovered the right kind of material, he still suffered setbacks.

One day in 1879, Edison got the idea to try a carbonized cotton fiber. He worked for five hours to make the fiber, only to have it break in two before he removed the mold. He then spent the next several hours going through two spools of cotton thread to find the perfect strand, only to ruin it when he tried to place it in a glass tube. He then spent the next two days without sleep trying to slip one of the carbonized threads into a vacuum-sealed bulb. But all of his hard work paid off when he flipped the switch and saw the glow of electric current.

How's that for commitment? Do you doubt that Edison would have continued had that last attempt failed – or even the next one? It's pretty obvious that he would have conducted experiment after experiment *until* he succeeded. And that really is the magic word – "until."

There is nothing that is impossible for the man or woman who says, "I will not quit until I succeed." And the good news is that we were all born with this "never say die" spirit. If you don't believe me, then just watch babies learning to walk. They pull themselves to a standing position, only to fall almost immediately. They do it again and again and again. Finally, they are able to stand in a somewhat wobbly manner, but as soon as they start to move forward, they invariably fall again. After weeks or months of practice, they finally learn to walk, but even then, they continue to fall.

We could learn a lot from babies. For one, they aren't embarrassed by their failures. They seem to possess enough self-esteem to know that they don't have to be perfect at something to start. As adults, we seem to forget this concept and focus only on those things that we already do well.

FAIL OFTEN

Secondly, babies seem to understand that the best way to do something well is to first do it poorly. The time it takes for a baby to learn to walk can vary by months from child to child. But the real determining factor is simply practice. The babies who relentlessly pull themselves back up and start again are the ones who learn to walk first. The same will be true in the pursuit of your dream. Thomas Watson, founder of IBM, once said, "The way to accelerate your success is to double your failure rate."

This principle is wonderfully illustrated in the world of sports. For instance, in baseball, the players who hit the most home runs are also those who strike out the most. Hank Aaron, Mickey Mantle and Babe Ruth were all career strikeout leaders, as well as home run leaders. In fact, Barry Bonds, who currently holds the record for the most home runs in a season, also holds the record for the most strikeouts in a season.

> **"The man who does not make mistakes does not usually make anything."**
> **—Bishop W. C. Magee**

ONE VICTORY IS ENOUGH

As you can see, the people who enjoy greatest success are those who also endure the greatest failure. The sad truth is that failure is much more common in life than success. Think about it. We fail in romantic relationships much more often than we succeed in them. Most of us fail in several relationships before we eventually find the right person. However, if you've been blessed with a happy, long-term relationship like I have, then you know that one success is enough.

All you really need is one success to make you forget about all the failures before it. For instance, 23 publishers rejected Dr. Seuss' first children's book. However, the 24th publisher sold six million copies of his work. Do you think Dr. Seuss spent many nights crying over the first 23 rejections? Or do you think that Alex Haley is upset that before *Roots* he wrote dozens of articles and stories that were never published?

TAKE ONE MORE STEP

The key factor for any winner in the race of life is to learn to persevere through the inevitable failures that litter the road to success. Often, the difference between winning and losing is simply the ability to hold on – the ability to take one more step. For instance, water heated to 211 degrees is simply hot water. It can be used for cooking or washing clothes. However, if you add just one more degree of temperature, you can use that same water to propel a train across the country or a ship across the ocean. Just one tiny degree makes a big difference.

Remember, the race is not always won by the fastest runner, but sometimes by the runner who just keeps running. This is illustrated in a classic story called "The Pebble of Success." In 1942, according to legend, an exploration crew went to Venezuela in search of diamonds. Over the next several months, they failed to find any sign of valuable diamonds and soon became discouraged. One day, while mining in a dry river bed, Rafael Solano announced, "I've had it! See this pebble? This makes the 999,999th one that I've picked up without finding a single diamond. I quit!"

A crewman said, "Why not make it an even million? Pick up another." Rafael thought to himself, "Why not?" He reached down and picked up a large stone. The stone not only turned out to be a diamond, but also the largest and purest diamond ever found. It's reported that a New York jeweler paid Solano $200,000 for the stone. And remember, this was in the 1940s.

When you experience failure in life, remember that the next stone you pick up could be the one that makes all the difference. When I experience failures in my own life, I simply try to keep in mind the words of Rudyard Kipling:

> *If you can force your heart and nerve and sinew*
> *To serve your turn long after they are gone,*
> *And so hold on when there is nothing in you*
> *Except the Will which says to them: "Hold on!"*

THE MYTH OF FAILURE

Of course, one thing that may help you to hold on is to change your thoughts about failure. For most of this chapter, I've used the term "failure" in an effort to get you comfortable with the concept that things will not always go your way. However, the truth is that there is no such thing as "failure." In any situation, you achieve one of two results – success or some other result that can later lead to success.

Perhaps no one has ever understood this concept better than Thomas Edison. After his 13-month ordeal to invent the incandescent light bulb, he was interviewed by a young reporter who asked, "Mr. Edison, how does it feel to have failed 10,000 times trying to invent the light bulb?" Edison looked sternly at the reporter and said, "Young man, I didn't fail 10,000 times trying to invent the light bulb. I simply found 10,000 ways that didn't work!"

As you can see, Edison embraced the concept of failure. He treated each failure as a learning experience. Whenever one attempt didn't work, he recorded his *results* and tried a new approach. And this is a very important thing to understand – he tried something *different*. Had Edison simply tried the same thing over and over, we may still be sitting in the dark today.

Insanity is trying the same thing over and over and expecting a different approach. Therefore, when you make a second or third (or 300th attempt) at making the sale, getting the job, getting married or whatever, make sure that you vary your approach. Relentlessness is important but it must be coupled with flexibility.

You never fail in life – you simply gain experience. Someone once said that "Experience is what you get when you don't get what you want." And as you know, experience is valuable. In fact, when was the last time that you saw a help wanted ad that said, "No experience preferred"? Often, it's only through experience that you can learn the lessons required. Do you think you could learn to swim by reading a book about swimming? If so, would you be confident enough to jump into the deep end of a pool after reading the last page? I doubt it. You only truly learn to swim by getting in the water, thrashing about and inadvertently swallowing half of the pool. As Aristotle said, "What we have to learn to do, we learn by doing." But, although we learn best this way, it shouldn't stop you from learning through other sources – books, tapes and training materials. All can give you crucial knowledge that will help speed up the learning process.

EMBRACE OBSTACLES

However, in the final analysis, you can only reach your destination by making the journey yourself – a journey with obstacles. Before I understood the beauty of obstacles, I would decry anything in my path as "unfair." Like most young men, I was extremely impatient. I wanted to have it all right now, even if "right now" was not the right time for me. And my impatience led to a number of downfalls.

Now that I am older and (hopefully) wiser, I've learned to embrace obstacles. I know that within every obstacle is the opportunity to grow and stretch my wings. My obstacles have been my greatest blessings. Even my incarceration was a blessing in disguise. I often tell people that I was not arrested but *rescued*. If I hadn't been incarcerated and forced to take time to reflect on my actions, I truly believe that I would be dead today.

As Homer said, "Adversity has the effect of eliciting talents which in prosperous circumstances would have lain dormant." For instance, there is a story of a man who wanted to have the four-foot deep basement of his home dug out a full eight feet to accommodate a laundry room and gym.

There was no way to get equipment into the basement, so he hired manual laborers to remove the dirt with five-gallon buckets and a rope through the original coal chute. On the fifth day, the lead digger approached him with a problem— they had dug around a huge rock in the middle of the floor. It was about five feet in diameter and was one of those very smooth rocks that couldn't be chipped with a sledgehammer.

The man called in an engineer who suggested that they could drill into the center with a carbon drill, place a very small amount of dynamite inside, and crack the rock into small enough pieces to carry it up the coal chute. However, it would cost $2,800. Another contractor wanted to bring in a pneumatic air hammer. His price was *only* $2,200. The rock had to go, but what was the right way to get rid of it?

Suddenly, the man had a thought: He asked his lead digger how long it would take to dig a hole six feet by six feet right next to the rock. He said, "Three hours." At $10 an hour, the man gave him the go-ahead. When the hole was dug, they simply pushed the rock into the hole. It completely vanished at a total cost of $30. The basement turned out as beautifully and functionally finished as planned. In the process, he saved more than $2,000. However, the lesson he learned in being resourceful was probably worth even more. Obstacles can be blessings.

"When trouble moves in, make it pay the rent."
—Unknown

In fact, in some cases, we can only make it to our destination if we have a burden to carry. For instance, if you were trying to cross a swift-moving stream, you would be in danger of being knocked off your feet and swept away in the current. The best way to avoid this is to find a large stone (the heavier the better) and carry it across the stream on your shoulders as a ballast. The extra weight of the stone would keep your feet solidly planted on the bed of the stream and prevent disaster.

Ann Landers was once asked what she thought the most useful advice was for all of humanity. Here is her answer:

Expect trouble as an inevitable part of life, and when it comes, hold your head high, look it squarely in the eye and say, "I will be bigger than you. You cannot defeat me."

Now that's good advice!

Brace Yourself

I am, by nature, an optimist. I look for, and usually find, the best in every person, situation, or event, and I try to pass on this optimism to everyone I meet. However, being an optimist does not blind me from the realities of the world, and neither should it blind you.

The reality is that not everyone is going to be supportive of your efforts to make the most of your DASH. As you move out of the shadows and take your rightful place in the sun, you will be subjected to the blistering sting of criticism. And perhaps, most painful of all, this criticism will often come from the people closest to you—friends and loved ones. They will say things like, "Who is she to think she can do that?" or "Why does he think that he's better than us?" or "She's changed! She's no fun anymore!"

I wish I could tell you that you will be exempt from these types of attacks, but I doubt you will. Every person who has ever achieved greatness has suffered the "slings and arrows of outrageous fortune." For instance, when Christopher Columbus departed on his fateful journey to the New World, do you think everyone was in his corner? Of course not. There were those who said, "Why can't you be satisfied with the half of the world that we know about now? You must think that you're smarter than the rest of us. You'll get what you deserve when you sail right off the edge of the earth."

Similar words were muttered to Dr. Martin Luther King when he began his fight for racial equality. Today, Dr. King has a holiday when millions of people pay tribute to him, but this was not always the case. During the 1960s, many people thought Dr. King was a "trouble maker." He was called arrogant and unrealistic. He has been accused of everything from plagiarism to infidelity. But, fortunately for all of us, he persisted and, in the process, made America a better place for all of us to live.

Now surely if a man as great as Dr. King was criticized, discouraged, and even lied about, what can the rest of us expect to encounter in our DASH through destiny? My friends, we can expect the same treatment. And considering that most of us are more blameworthy than Dr. King (I know I am) we can expect more of it. So brace yourself for the storm and determine within yourself that you will keep trudging forward, no matter how hard the winds of criticism, the rain of doubt, and the hail of gossip.

"The best revenge is massive success."

Frank Sinatra

THOUGHTS FOR YOUR DASH

Determination
> "What counts is not necessarily the size of the dog in the fight—it's the size of the fight in the dog."
> DWIGHT D. EISENHOWER

Attitude
> "You must begin to think of yourself as becoming the person you want to be."
> DAVID VISCOTT

Success
> "The truth is there are only two things in life: reasons and results. And reasons simply don't count."
> DR. ROBERT ANTHONY

Happiness
> "Joy is not in things, it is in us."
> RICHARD WAGNER

CHAPTER 19

The Fear Factor

Life will put several obstacles in your path – if you're lucky. But no obstacle will be greater than *you*. There is an African proverb that says, "If there is no enemy within, then the enemy outside can do us no harm." And if you are like most of us, then the biggest internal enemy that you will have to deal with is fear.

Each year, heart disease and cancer combine to claim the lives of more than 1 million people. However, fear kills many more each year. In recent years, researchers have found that stress plays a large role in several of the leading causes of death in America, including heart disease and cancer. More importantly, fear prevents many more people from ever living in the first place.

Fear keeps many of us chained to jobs that don't stimulate us or demand the most of our talents. Fear keeps us locked in relationships that are toxic and draining the very life from us. Fear can be a more powerful jail than Alcatraz, Sing Sing and Leavenworth *combined*. And this is the case whether your fears are real or imagined.

CONDITIONED FEAR

Have you ever been to the zoo and noticed that the elephant is usually tethered in its pen by a small chain around his leg? This chain is often secured to a bolt or sometimes, just a small wooden peg. If so, you've probably asked yourself, "How does that flimsy restraint keep a 3-ton animal in his pen?" Well, the truth of the matter is that the restraint doesn't keep him in the pen. Fear does.

After a baby elephant is born in the zoo, the handlers place a sturdy metal clasp around one of its ankles and tie it to a heavy metal chain that is bolted into the ground. As the baby elephant moves around its holding area, it will occasionally go too far and pull against the heavily bolted chain. This causes the baby elephant some pain, and before long, the elephant learns to judge how far it can safely move around in its surroundings without feeling the jerk of the chain. Surprisingly, as the elephant grows bigger and stronger, its restraints are lessened rather than increased because by that time, the elephant is too *afraid* to test the strength of the chain.

People are similar to elephants in this manner. Let's suppose your parents had you on a very tight leash. In an effort to protect you from harm, they controlled your environment and kept you close to them. Whenever you did manage to stray, you were punished or sternly lectured. Over time, you learned just how far you could safely go outside of their circle of influence while staying within the boundaries.

If this was your childhood experience, then you may be limiting yourself like the mighty elephant. You may be working in a field that your parents thought was acceptable. You may be in a relationship with a person who meets your parents' idea of a "nice boy" or "nice girl." Or you may only engage in activities that your parents did when they were your age. In short, you may be tethered by chains of disapproval, criticism or shame.

The point is not for us to start playing the "blame game" with our parents. In most cases, our parents did the best job of raising us the best way they knew how to do. In fact, if you were overly protected, it was probably because they sincerely and truly loved you and wanted the best for you.

Instead, the point here is to give you an opportunity to do what the elephant cannot – reflect on your situation in light of your *current* circumstances. If the adult elephant could do so, it would realize that it could easily break the chains. However, it has been conditioned through fear not to even try.

In a sense, we all have been conditioned through fear. And this is not always bad. For instance, if you ever touched a hot stove, then you don't have to be told not to do it again. This is a good thing and will save you from future pain or injury. The only drawback is that you may also be afraid to touch a *cold* stove.

FACING YOUR FEARS

Fear is a powerful force, and unfortunately, it isn't always rational. So the first step is to examine your fears. Are they real fears or simply imagined? One way to do that is to pull on your "chains" a little bit. Give them a tug. As Shakespeare's Julius Caesar said, "Cowards die many times before their deaths. The valiant never taste of death but once."

There is a story of a little boy who learned this lesson in dealing with his fear of a dog. Each day, on his way home from school, a big dog chased this little boy home. One day, the little boy simply got tired of running away and decided he would stand his ground. The next day, the little boy found himself being chased by the dog. However, instead of running as usual, the boy stopped and picked up a stick.

As the dog came closer, the boy noticed an amazing thing – the dog didn't have any teeth. The boy realized that for months he had been running from the dog for fear of being *gummed* to death. However, when he stood up to his fear, he learned that Franklin Roosevelt was right; "There is nothing to fear but fear itself." It's time for us to act like this courageous little boy. We must start to ask, "What am I running from, and does it have teeth that will do me any harm?"

Sort Your Fears

The other question we must ask is "Can I keep this fear and still get to where I want to go?" We don't need to alleviate all fears from our lives to be successful, just those fears that hold us back.

For instance, my wife is afraid of the ocean. No matter how many times I try to talk her into scuba diving with me, it isn't going to happen. I can take her to a pool, teach her how to use the equipment, show her all of the do's and don'ts, but when it's time to jump into the ocean, she won't go. Why? Because it isn't necessary for her to learn scuba diving for her to be a great artist, wife and mother. She has decided to keep that fear *for now* and that's fine.

In fact, I would encourage you to keep some of your fears as well. If you are afraid of drugs, alcohol or cigarettes, these are all healthy fears. On the other hand, there are certain fears that we must all confront, such as the fear of rejection. It will be impossible to reach your destination in life without encountering a little rejection. It's part of the process. Not everyone will agree with your idea for a new product, service, day care center, school for the deaf or whatever it is you want to accomplish with your dash.

However, to reach the people who will support your dream, you must knock on a lot of doors, and some of those will come crashing back in your face. Knowing this, you will be paralyzed from ever taking action if you keep your fear of rejection.

Reverse Your Fears

One way to take the sting out of fear is by reversing your fears. Instead of being afraid to do something, be afraid NOT to do it. Be afraid NOT to go back to school. Be afraid NOT to ask for the promotion. Be afraid NOT to ask for the date. Do this by simply focusing on the costs of NOT taking action. After all, as a youth league hockey coach once told Wayne Gretzky, "You miss 100 percent of the shots you never take."

For instance, a young man may meet a pretty girl and want to ask her out on a date. However, his internal conversation will say, "What if she says 'No'? That sure will hurt. Let's not take the chance." The way to counteract this fear of rejection is to reverse the internal dialogue: "What if I miss out on the chance to marry the woman of my dreams because of my fear of being turned down? That will hurt a lot more. Let's do it!"

The pain we suffer from failing is seldom as great as the rewards we gain from success. In fact, one of the questions I've learned to ask myself when I'm confronted with fear is "What's the worst thing that can happen to me, and if it does, will I die?" If the answer is "yes," then it's time to re-evaluate the importance of my goal. However, in most cases, the worst-case scenario is not death and in that case, I go for it. Nietzsche said, "What doesn't kill me only makes me stronger!" So, at the very least, by going for it, I become stronger.

Do It Anyway

> **"Act brave. The world steps aside for the man
> who acts like he knows where he is going."**
> **—D. S. Jordan**

Another way to handle your fear is to take the advice of Susan Jeffers' best-selling book, *Feel the Fear and Do It Anyway*.

Is this an easy thing to do? No. It takes courage. But contrary to popular belief, courage is not the absence of fear. Courage is the ability to take action in spite of fear. And courage, like any other character trait, can be acquired through practice.

In fact, learning to exercise your courage is much like learning to exercise a muscle. When you start, it's a struggle. This is particularly true if your courage has atrophied due to years of neglect. The key is to build your courage up slowly like you would a muscle. For instance, if you haven't exercised in years, you wouldn't try to do Arnold Schwarzenegger's workout your first time out. Instead, you'd start with something easier and work your way up.

You should take the same approach to exercising your courage. For instance, let's suppose you have a fear of investing in the stock market. Over the years, you have convinced yourself (or been convinced) that only the professionals can make money in the market and that novices like yourself are bound to lose their shirts.

In working on this fear, I wouldn't suggest taking your entire life savings and dumping it into the market. That wouldn't be courageous; that would be *courazy*! What I would suggest is that you take a tiny amount of money (even as little as $100) and open up a brokerage account over the internet. As you get more comfortable as a stock market investor, you could add more money to your account. The point is to start small and build up your courage "muscle."

Eleanor Roosevelt summed this up perfectly when she said:

"You gain strength, courage and confidence by every experience in which you really stop to look fear in the face. You are able to say to yourself, 'I lived through this horror. I can take the next thing that comes along.' You must do the thing you think you cannot do."

TAKING RISKS

Most of us are risk-averse. We simply aren't comfortable with the thought of putting our money, our health, our relationships or anything else of value *at risk*. However, as you know, risk is absolutely necessary. To achieve success, we must risk failure. As Will Rogers once said, "You've got to go out on a limb sometimes, because that's where the fruit is."

In fact, without risk, your dash will be as unremarkable as Miss Jones, an elderly spinster who lived in a Midwestern town. As the story goes, upon her death, the editor at the local newspaper was perplexed about what to write in her obituary. She had never been married, had children or done anything of note (good or bad). Having trouble finding anything suitable to say about her, he decided to assign the story to the next reporter who came into his office, who happened to be a young sports reporter. Here is what this reporter wrote about Miss Jones in her obituary:

> *Here lies the bones of Nancy Jones*
> *For her life held no terrors.*
> *She lived an old maid. She died an old maid.*
> *No hits, no runs, no errors.*

How would you like that on your tombstone? Well, the only way to avoid such a fate is to re-evaluate your attitude towards risk. David Lloyd George said, "Don't be afraid to take a big step if one is indicated. You can't cross a chasm in two small jumps." I've been able to do this by redefining the concept. I now view risk as an acronym for "Research, Invest, Strategize and Keep" the critics away.

Research. By gathering all relevant information and assessing your probabilities of success and failure, you can turn

209

blind risk into calculated risk. We can all live with calculated risk. In fact, we take these risks whenever we buy a house, accept a job offer or get married.

Invest. You should know upfront that any action will require an investment on your part, even if it's just an investment of time. Make sure that you include the "costs" into your calculations so you aren't unpleasantly surprised by the outcome of your decision.

Strategize. Be sure to develop an entry strategy and, perhaps more importantly, an exit strategy. What are the exact steps you need to take in order to succeed? How can you minimize your loss if things don't go as planned? The latter question is extremely important because things seldom work out as planned. In those cases, you should have a contingency plan.

As you know, an unfortunate example of this occurred on the maiden (and only) voyage of the Titanic. The ship wasn't equipped with enough lifeboats in case of disaster. As a result, hundreds of people died who otherwise would have been saved, had the ship's owner planned for the worst-case scenario.

Keep the Critics Away. This may be the most important step in the risk process. There will be plenty of people who will believe that your dream is impossible. They will swear it can't be done. Just as people swore that no one could run a mile in less than four minutes or swim the English Channel or create a heavier than air flying machine. The best way to deal with these people is to keep in mind the words of this Edgar Guest poem:

IT COULDN'T BE DONE

Somebody said that it couldn't be done,
But he with a chuckle replied
That "maybe it couldn't," but he would be one
Who wouldn't say so till he'd tried.
So he buckled right in with the trace of a grin
On his face. If he worried he hid it.
He started to sing as he tackled the thing
That couldn't be done, and he did it.

Somebody scoffed: "Oh, you'll never do that.
At least no one ever has done it";
But he took off his coat and he took off his hat,
And the first thing we knew he'd begun it.
With a lift of his chin and a bit of a grin,
Without any doubting or quiddit,
He started to sing as he tackled the thing
That couldn't be done, and he did it.

There are thousands to tell you it cannot be done,
There are thousands to prophesy failure;
There are thousands to point out to you, one by one,
The dangers that wait to assail you.
But just buckle in with a bit of a grin,
Just take off your coat and go to it;
Just start to sing as you tackle the thing
That "cannot be done," and you'll do it.

Conquering Your Fear Factor

Each week, on the TV show, *Fear Factor*, a group of contestants competes in a series of frightening stunts for $50,000 in cash. Many of the stunts require them to perform tasks while being suspended high in the air or submerged in water. However, by far, the most difficult stunts involve insects and snakes. In some stunts, the contestants are required to eat live insects and in other stunts, the contestants must climb into a tank crawling with snakes or be covered from head to toe with bees.

And although fear gets the best of some contestants causing them to drop out of the competition, a surprising number of contestants continue on in the competition. Now, you may wonder what would make someone subject themselves to such fearful circumstances. However, the answer comes down to one simple reason. Actually, it comes down to 50,000 reasons—the money.

These people have a direct payoff in mind when they step into a tank of sharks or agree to eat a bucket of pig intestines. This payoff allows them to work beyond their fear and discomfort because the end result—$50,000—is greater than their temporary discomfort. In essence, they focus on the rewards and not on the fear.

Well, if you want to conquer *your* fear factor, you must do the same thing. For example, if fear is preventing you from starting your own business, it's because you're paying too much attention to the downside of starting your own business—not having a stable paycheck, the difficulty of getting funded, dealing with employees and customers, etc. And trust me, as someone who has run several businesses, these are legitimate fears. Yet, they pale in comparison to the benefits of running a successful business—the feeling of pride and accomplishment, the freedom to set your own schedule, the ability to set your own goals and priorities, the possibility of becoming super wealthy, etc.

The simple truth of the matter is that what you have to gain by starting your own business dwarfs what you have to lose. And this is the same with almost everything. What you have to gain by losing weight or quitting smoking is far greater than the short-term pain you'll endure in the process. What you have to gain by submitting your poetry to a publisher or entering your prized cabbage at the county fair greatly surpasses what you have to lose by being rejected.

Yet, sadly, many people allow fear to hold them hostage because they focus on the wrong side of the equation. In a sense, they're looking into a microscope instead of through a telescope. Therefore, instead of seeing the massive opportunities that lie in front of them, they magnify the tiny obstacles in their path.

Interestingly, Arnold Schwarzenegger talked about this phenomenon once in an interview. He was explaining his transformation from B-movie actor to mega superstar. He said, "One day, I realized that I was looking at life through the wrong end of the telescope and it was up to me to turn it around and make everything bigger and brighter." I think this statement applies to most of us. So many people are living beneath their privilege because they've taken the wrong perspective on life. Instead of focusing on the possibilities, they focus on the problems.

This is what the contestants on *Fear Factor* do and they're only competing for $50,000. In all likelihood, you're competing for a lot more. You have the opportunity to make all of your dreams come true. And more importantly, you have the opportunity to make the most of your DASH—to accomplish your destiny. With all that to gain, surely you can look past your fears and toward your future.

"Even though you may want to move forward in your life, you may have one foot on the brakes. In order to be free, we must learn how to let go. Release the hurt. Release the fear. Refuse to entertain your old pain. The energy it takes to hang onto the past is holding you back from a new life. What is it you would let go of today?"

Mary Manin Morrissey

THOUGHTS FOR YOUR DASH

Determination
> "Courage is not the absence of fear, but rather the judgment that something else is more important than fear."
>
> AMBROSE REDMOON

Attitude
> "If what you're working for really matters, you'll give it all you've got."
>
> NIDO QUBEIN

Success
> "Don't measure yourself by what you have accomplished, but by what you should have accomplished with your ability."
>
> JOHN WOODEN

Happiness
> "Only one thing has to change for us to know happiness in our lives: where we focus our attention."
>
> GREG ANDERSON

CHAPTER 20

The Buck Stops Here

One of the most valuable traits any person can possess is the ability to assume responsibility. When a person takes responsibility for something in life, he or she says, "This thing is going to happen because *I* am going to make it happen." The ability to make this type of statement and then, more importantly, to carry it out, will largely determine the significance of your dash.

It can also make you *rich*. In many large companies, the CEO makes as much as a thousand times more than the entry-level employee in the mailroom. But why? Surely the CEO doesn't work a thousand times more hours. Nor is the CEO a thousand times smarter. So why is the CEO compensated so well?

Because that person is ultimately *responsible* for the fate of the company. If the company has a few bad quarters, the board of directors isn't going to ask for the mailroom clerk's resignation; it's going to ask for CEO's resignation. On the other hand, if the company does well, then it will be the CEO (and not the mailroom clerk) who gets stock options worth millions.

Of course, the corporate world isn't the only place where taking responsibility pays off. In every area of life, the person who takes responsibility for his actions and the results they produce generally makes the most out of their dash. As Ben Stein once said, "Nothing happens by itself ... It all will come your way, once you understand that you have to *make it* come your way, by your own exertions."

A successful business doesn't "just happen." You have to make it happen. And the same thing applies to a successful marriage, a successful friendship or a successful relationship with your Creator. We've all heard the expression that "money doesn't grow on trees." And surely this is true. However, even if money did grow on trees, somebody would have to climb up the tree and bring the money down. In short, nothing *worthwhile* just happens. If you want the good stuff in life, you're going to have to work for it.

TAKE RESPONSIBILITY FOR YOUR ATTITUDE

In his classic poem *Invictus*, British poet William Henley writes:

> *Out of the night that covers me,*
> *Black as the pit from pole to pole,*
> *I thank whatever gods may be*
> *For my unconquerable soul.*

> *It matters not how strait the gate,*
> *How charged with punishments the scroll,*
> *I am the master of my fate:*
> *I am the captain of my soul.*

Interestingly, Henley wrote this poem while confined for 20 months in an infirmary suffering from tuberculosis. During the ordeal, he had to have his foot amputated. Though he may have lost a foot, he didn't lose his "unconquerable soul." Henley's health was eventually restored, and he went on to live an active life as one of England's premier literary figures of the 19th century.

We could all learn a thing or two from Henley's story. Though we may not always be able to control our circumstances, we can always control our attitude toward them. In that sense, we are all masters of our fates and the captains of our souls.

I wish I could have said the same thing about my life. As a young man, I blamed everything and everyone for my problems. I blamed my parents for not protecting me from abuse. I blamed my father for disrupting my teenage years. I blamed my teachers and guidance counselors for not giving me the proper training. I blamed nature for not making me smart enough.

Of course, all of this blame didn't do a single thing for me. It didn't put food on the table or a roof over my head. It didn't give me strength and courage to face my problems. And it certainly didn't build several multi-million dollar businesses and find me the woman of my dreams. What did turn my life around was taking responsibility for myself and taking the actions necessary to transform my life.

In the words of Jesse Jackson, "Both tears and sweat are salty, but they render a different result. Tears will get you sympathy, sweat will get you change." In short, my life changed the moment I said, "The buck stops here."

TAKE RESPONSIBILITY FOR YOUR DECISIONS

It's often said that the quality of our lives is a direct result of the quality of our decisions. This has certainly been true in my case. I've made some wonderful decisions that have added love, beauty and abundance to my life and I've made some horrendous decisions that have brought pain not only to me, but also to my loved ones.

I've often looked back and said, "If I only knew then what I know now." We all wish for a crystal ball in our lives from time to time. Of course, no such crystal ball exists, nor would it be a blessing if it did. After all, isn't part of the fun in life the fact that we don't know what the future holds? How fun is it to watch a movie or a sporting event that you've already seen? Life is about making choices about an unknown future. In the classic poem, *The Road Less Traveled*, Robert Frost writes:

> *Two roads diverged in a yellow wood*
> *And sorry I could not travel both*
> *And be one traveler, long I stood*
> *And looked down one as far as I could*
> *To where it bent in the undergrowth*
>
> *Then took the other as just as fair*
> *And having perhaps the better claim*
> *Because it was grassy and wanted wear*
> *Though as for that, the passing there*
> *Had worn them really about the same*
>
> *And both that morning equally lay*
> *In leaves no step had trodden black*
> *Oh, I kept the first for another day!*
> *Yet, knowing how way leads onto way*
> *I doubted if I should ever come back*
>
> *I shall be telling this with a sigh*
> *Somewhere ages and ages hence*
> *Two roads diverged in a wood*
> *And I took the one less traveled by*
> *And that has made all the difference*

We are all like Robert Frost in some way. We come to certain junctures in life, where we must make a choice to go one way or another. Like Frost, we try to look as far into the future as possible. However, our vision is necessarily limited so we head down one road tentatively, thinking that we can always go back and head down the other road if this one doesn't work out. However, that is seldom the case because the current road splits again and again, and before long, we can't find our way back to the original fork in the road. Even if we could find our way back, it would take days, weeks or years to do so.

In the end, some lives become a collection of "If only I had taken that job in Chicago," "If only I had married Bill instead of Steve," "If only I had spent more time with my children when they were little," – the list goes on and on. Of course, all of those "if onlys" are just a waste of time. None of us can turn back the clock. The only thing that we can do is try to make better decisions in the future.

And one way to do so is to SLOW DOWN. There is an old builder's maxim that says "Measure twice, cut once." By carefully planning your actions *beforehand*, you can save a tremendous amount of effort down the road. I suggest that when you are confronted with a big decision, you take the following actions:

·*Get all the facts*
·*Describe the problem in detail*
·*List all possible solutions*
·*List the advantages and disadvantages of each*
·*Detail what you will do*
·*Follow through*

By doing so, you can avoid the actions of a famous American general on June 25, 1876. When he received information that a significant number of Indians were gathering, he decided to take action without obtaining all of the facts or analyzing them. As a result, he wound up riding out with 250 men to "surround" almost 3,000 Indians. Unfortunately for General George Armstrong Custer and the rest of his men at the battle of Little Big Horn, this proved to be a fatal mistake.

Know Your Worth

On Easter Sunday 1976, Bertha Adams, a seventy-one-year-old West Palm Beach woman, died of malnutrition. At the time of her death, Bertha weighed just fifty pounds. When authorities investigated the situation, they learned that she had been living hand-to-mouth and on several occasions, had resorted to begging her neighbors for food. A visit to her home revealed that Bertha had lived the life of penniless recluse. Her home was in shambles but amongst the debris, they found two keys to safety deposit boxes at two different banks. So you can imagine the shock and dismay the authorities felt when they discovered more than $1 million worth of stock certificates and cash tucked away in those boxes.

Apparently, Bertha had been unaware of the contents of these boxes. As a result, she died in poverty when she could have lived in luxury. Many of the investigators wondered how such a thing could happen. However, in my travels as a speaker and personal coach, I know all too well how such a thing can happen. In fact, I encounter people similar to this little old lady every day.

These people possess an abundance of potential, yet they live with scarcity. They have just enough money to make it through the month although they have skills and talents worth millions. They experience just enough joy and satisfaction although they are surrounded with a multitude of friends and loved ones. They barely have enough energy to make it through the day although they have every reason to be enthusiastic of about their lives. In short, these people live well beneath their privilege and for just the same reason that Bertha did—they don't know the treasures they have in store.

Sadly, we all have a little Bertha inside of us. I know that I did. Although I made my first fortune as a relatively young man, I could have done it even earlier. I spent a few years floundering from one job to the other until I found one of my keys—the ability to motivate and inspire. And even after I "made it," I still didn't realize the worth of what I had attained. If I had, I would have never thrown it all away chasing a few extra bucks. But that is precisely the kind of thing people do when they don't realize what they have.

Do you know what you have? And before you answer with a perfunctory "yes," take a moment to think about it. Have you taken a complete inventory of you—your skills, your talents, your friends, your connections, your sense of humor, you character, your health, *everything*? If you're like most people, you'll probably realize that you've undervalued your worth; and not just from a monetary standpoint. And sadly, when you don't fully appreciate your value, then you don't place enough value on your care and treatment.

Locked inside you are all the wealth, happiness, contentment, fulfillment, and love that you could ever want or need. The important thing is to find the key that will unlock these treasures in you and then USE IT. Tap into those treasures and make a difference in your DASH and the DASHes of others. And whatever you do, don't sell yourself short. Know your worth.

"Have the daring to accept yourself as a bundle of possibilities and undertake the game of making the most of your best."

Henry Emerson Fosdick

THOUGHTS FOR YOUR DASH

Determination

"Four steps to achievement: Plan purposefully. Prepare prayerfully. Proceed positively. Pursue persistently."

WILLIAM A. WARD

Attitude

"Optimists are right. So are pessimists. It's up to you to choose which you will be."

HARVEY MACKAY

Success

"The greats often became great because they continued to believe in themselves despite apparent failures."

MICHAEL GELB AND TONY BUZAN

Happiness

"Happiness and misery depend not on how high up or low down you are—they depend not upon these, but on the direction in which you are tending."

SAMUEL BUTLER

CHAPTER 21

Money Matters

As I speak to groups around the country, the one issue that comes up time and time again is money – namely, how to make more of it. There seems to be an almost universal thirst for money, and much of it is misplaced.

For one, many people tend to think that money is a "wonder drug." I constantly hear comments like "If I had more money, I'd start a business" or "If I had more money, I'd contribute to worthy causes." In other words, if they had more money, they'd be different people. Nothing could be further from the truth.

> **"Make no mistake, my friend, it takes more than money to make men rich."**
> **—A. P. Gouthey**

Remember what we discussed earlier about what happens to people who miraculously come into money? In a short time, they are broke again and no better off as a result of the experience. Money won't give you any qualities that you don't already possess, and money won't make you happy.

If you don't believe me, then just read the entertainment or sports section of your daily newspaper. There you will read about people who have all the money in the world but are dealing with drug and alcohol addictions, divorce and other legal problems.

Of course, I'm not suggesting that entertainers and athletes are any more prone to these problems than the rest of us. I'm simply pointing out that having money doesn't provide you with immunity from life's problems. Money is simply a tool, and as such, the important thing to remember is to use money and not let money use you.

MONEY IS A TOOL

This seems like a rather obvious statement, but from my experience I've learned that money uses us much more than we use it. For instance, millions of people get up every morning and go to jobs they hate. This isn't because they are masochists or can't figure out anything better to do. Instead, they are simply trying to make a living the best way they know how. Instead of using money to enhance their lives, they are diminishing their lives for the sake of money.

This is unfortunate because they're not only draining the life from their years, but also the years from their lives. According to research, the most common time for someone to have a heart attack is between 8 a.m. and 9 a.m. on Monday morning. As you know, this is the hour that most people go back to work after the weekend. I don't think that this is a coincidence. If you sell your life to make money, you will likely end up with neither.

There is a Chinese fable about an old woodcutter who went into the mountains almost every day to cut wood. It was said that this old man was a miser who hoarded his silver until it changed to gold, and that he cared more for gold than anything else in the world.

One day while out cutting wood, a tiger jumped from the brush and carried him off in his mouth. The woodcutter's son saw his father's danger, and ran to save him. Soon, he caught up with the tiger and noticed that his father was not hurt much because the tiger held him by his clothes.

The woodcutter's son drew his knife to slay the tiger. When the old woodcutter saw his son about to stab the tiger, he called out in great alarm: "Do not spoil the tiger's skin! If you can kill him without cutting holes in his skin, we can get many pieces of silver for it. Kill him, but do not cut his body." While the son tried to think of a way to accomplish this, the tiger suddenly dashed off into the forest, carrying the old man where the son could not reach him, and he was soon killed.

Although this fable is centuries old, its lessons still apply today. Many of us are being carried off in the jaws of jobs that are literally killing us. However, we miss our chances to escape because we are so attached to the money.

Now, please don't misunderstand me. I'm not knocking the concept of work. Nor am I suggesting that you get up tomorrow morning and quit your job. What I am suggesting is that you take a serious look at the part money plays in your life. Are you doing what you do so you can continue to earn money, or are you earning money so that you can continue to do what you do? After all, money should be the servant and not the master.

One of my favorite jokes illustrates this problem. A man parked his brand new Mercedes alongside a curb and opened the door to get out. Just then, out of nowhere, a car came speeding past, knocking off his car door. A police officer arrived on the scene shortly thereafter to find the man ranting and raving about the damage done to his new car and oblivious to the fact that his arm had been severed in the accident. He simply kept shouting, "My Mercedes! My Mercedes!"

The officer said to the man, "You know, sir! I think you

should be less concerned about the damage to your car and more concerned about your arm." The man looked down at his arm, and noticing that it was gone, started shouting, "My Rolex! My Rolex!"

Of course, most of us aren't nearly so obsessed with money. However, I have to admit that for most of my life, money was my master. As a young man, I drifted from job to job trying to make a living. I'd get a job and work half-heartedly at it until I heard about another, higher paying job where I could again work half-heartedly. No matter how much more money I made each month, I never had anything to show for it.

The really intriguing thing about money is that you can't have it by chasing it. In this regard, it's like your shadow. You make a step or two toward it, and it moves away from you. You quicken your pace and it does the same. Even if you take off running after it, your shadow runs just as quickly, utterly refusing to give itself up. However, the moment you turn around and walk away from your shadow, it starts to run after you.

> **"You have reached the pinnacle of success as soon as you become uninterested in money, compliments or publicity."**
> **—Eddie Rickenbacker**

I found the same experience with money. Once I started concentrating on pursuing my passion, the money started chasing after me. This doesn't mean that I didn't plan to make *some* money. However, I ended up making much more money than I ever anticipated by not focusing on the money. Instead, I focused on using my gifts to bring about some reality I wanted to create, whether it was a new internet service or a new global positioning technology. In this way, money became my servant and not my master.

I truly believe that this is the path to success for most wealthy people, particularly the very wealthy. I don't imagine that Bill Gates sat around as a young man visualizing stacks of money. I imagine that instead he spent his time imagining a computer in every home, running the software that he would create. And by achieving this goal, he has earned more money than anyone in history.

In fact, I suspect that if Bill Gates had been focused on the money, he would have earned much less of it. He would have unnecessarily limited himself. This principle is best illustrated in a story about a farmer who took his family out for a Sunday drive. While they were out, a man delivered chickens to the farmer's house and left them in a crate on the front doorstep. When the family came home, the crate was open and chickens were running all over the lawn. The farmer and his family spent the next few hours chasing chickens.

That evening, the farmer called his chicken supplier and said, "How dare you leave the chickens in a crate on my front porch! They got out and my family had to run all over the neighborhood rounding them up. In fact, we only found 11 of them!" The supplier coolly responded, "Hey, 11 chickens isn't so bad, considering I only delivered 6!"

Obviously, the morale of this story is not to steal your neighbor's chickens. The lesson here is that you will usually get a lot more in life when you don't set an upper limit on your success.

Before I end this discussion on money, I want to take a moment to discuss both sides of the financial equation. Usually when we think of money, our question is "How do I make more of it?" Well, that is only half of the question. The other half is "How do I keep more of what I make?" Regardless of how much you make, if you spend all of what you make, you are still poor.

For instance, if someone makes $2 million each year, but

spends it all, he is still poor. It doesn't matter that he may drive a fancy car or have a nice home or even a yacht; he is still beholden to money. To keep what he has, he *must* continue to work. He is really no better off than the person who makes $15,000 each year and spends it all. In fact, I would argue that the man making $2 million is in worse shape.

This is a concept that took me years to understand, so let me try to explain it another way. Let's use a hypothetical example involving Suzy and Bill. Suzy and Bill graduate from the same college and start jobs in the same company making $50,000 a year. At the end of that first year, neither Suzy nor Bill has accumulated any savings. The next year, Suzy gets a raise to $60,000 but Bill's salary remains at $50,000. Once again, at the end of that year, neither Suzy nor Bill has accumulated any savings. This process continues for another four years and now Suzy makes $100,000 per year while Bill still makes only $50,000 annually. My question is "Who's better off from a financial point of view?"

The surprising answer is that Bill is better off. Bill's current lifestyle only requires $50,000 of annual income to sustain. However, Suzy's lifestyle requires $100,000 of annual income just to break even. Let's suppose that in the sixth year, the company they work for goes out of business. All things being equal, Bill is going to have a much easier time replacing his $50,000 salary than Suzy will have replacing her $100,000 salary.

For most of us, this seems counter-intuitive. Haven't we always been taught to make as much money as possible? Well, this is only true if we don't spend all of what we make. Let's suppose that instead of spending every penny she made, Suzy saved some of it. In the first year, she and Bill each saved $5,000 or 10 percent of their salaries. The next year, Bill saved $5,000 again but this time, Suzy saved $10,000 (the original $5,000 plus half of her raise). The next year, Bill saved $5,000 again and Suzy saved $15,000 ($10,000 plus half of her current year's raise). If this continues for six years, then their respective financial positions will be as depicted in the table below:

	BILL		SUZY	
	Spending	*Savings*	*Spending*	*Savings*
Year 1	$45,000	$5,000	$45,000	$5,000
Year 2	$45,000	$5,000	$50,000	$10,000
Year 3	$45,000	$5,000	$55,000	$15,000
Year 4	$45,000	$5,000	$60,000	$20,000
Year 5	$45,000	$5,000	$65,000	$25,000
Year 6	$45,000	$5,000	$70,000	$30,000
		$30,000		$105,000

As you can see, Bill will have accumulated $30,000 of savings and will be living off $45,000 per year. On the other hand, Suzy will have saved $105,000 and be living off $75,000 per year. Now, we can finally say that Suzy is better off than Bill.

In addition to living at a higher standard of living ($75,000 vs. $45,000), she also has a greater financial cushion. If the company goes out of business, she can live off her savings for about 18 months, while Bill only has eight months of living expenses saved. By not raising her lifestyle to the maximum limit of $100,000, she has a lot more flexibility in accepting new jobs, since she can live on $75,000. As you can see, it's not how much you earn, but rather what you do with what you earn.

Count All the Costs

I often identify with people who say that they are gradu-ates of the school of hard knocks. In fact, if such a school existed, I would not only be a graduate but a valedicto-rian as well. Time and again, I have had to learn lessons the hard way. One of those lessons occurred during my teenage years when I first began dating.

After nervously asking a girl out to dinner, I was amazed that she actually accepted my invitation. Be-cause I was working with a very limited budget, I didn't want to take any chances, so I called a local restaurant and to inquire about their prices. I asked for the price of the most expensive item on the menu, which was $15.95. I then thought to myself, "OK. $40 should cover it! Even if we both order the most expensive thing on the menu, that still leaves $8 left over for drinks."

You can probably guess what happened. My first surprise occurred when my date ordered an appetizer. Fortunately, I had built a little cushion into the budget by assuming the worst-case scenario, so I still felt that I had everything covered when she ordered a less expen-sive entrée. Nervously, while we ate and talked, I kept a running tally of the bill. At the end of dinner, my total stood at $38.90. I was able to dodge a bullet when my date passed on desert and for the first time that evening, I was able to relax and enjoy the date. That is until the bill arrived.

You can imagine my surprise when the actual bill came out to be $42.01 with the sales tax added in. U*h oh*! As I sat there wondering how I was going to make $2.01 magically appear in my wallet, my date asked, "Do you want me to pay the tip?" *The tip*? I hadn't even thought about a tip. Sheepishly, I had to agree, and then, to make matters worse, I had to "borrow" an additional $2.01 from her. She was gracious about the whole situation, but it was embarrassing nonetheless. That night, I learned an important lesson—count all the costs of any endeavor beforehand.

Now, before you start laughing at my naiveté in this situation, I want to remind you that you've probably had a similar situation in your own life. For instance, perhaps you set a budget of $2,000 for a new computer system. You went to a computer store and picked out your CPU, monitor, and printer with great care so that the total cost fit within your budget. However, you didn't figure in the costs of the sales tax, power cords, printer ink, etc. As a result, you walked out of the store having spent almost $2,500.

Or, perhaps you set a budget for a new car with monthly payments of up to $400 per month. However, you didn't count the costs of licensing, taxes, insurance, and warranties. As a result, your total cost of owning the car came out to be almost $600 per month. Or, perhaps you didn't count all the costs of home ownership or starting a business. The truth is that we are all guilty of not counting all the costs from time to time.

In fact, the biggest cost that we often fail to take into account is the cost to our relationships. When we get our hearts set on a new house or a new car, we often think that we can pay for this added expense by putting in extra time at work. We think, "I can afford this new house, if I just work one extra shift each week." Or we think, "I can start this business if I just work eighty hours per week for the first two years." However, we all too often fail to take into account just how those extra hours at the office or the plant will affect our relationships with our loved ones.

Therefore, we agree to take on extra projects at work in hope of getting a pay raise. We figure that we're willing to trade a few hours of extra effort for more money. However, we are trading more than just our efforts; we are trading our relationships with our loved ones when we are no longer available to coach our daughters' soccer team, help our sons with their homework, eat dinner with our families, etc.

Many times, the financial cost of obtaining the next possession is only a small percentage of the total cost. For some people, it becomes time to "pay the piper" when the kids go off to college. For others, the day of reckoning occurs only after the marriage has been damaged beyond repair. Only then do they realize the true costs of owning the BMW or the beach house or the speedboat.

Therefore, before you purchase that next car, computer system, set of golf clubs, or other toy, count all the costs of acquisition. Don't just focus on how much it will cost in terms of money. More importantly, how much will it cost in terms of time spent away from your loved ones? If you do that, you may discover (before it's too late) that the price is simply too high.

"Everything you want in life has a price connected to it. There's a price to pay if you want to make things better, a price to pay just for leaving things as they are, a price for everything."

Harry Browne

THOUGHTS FOR YOUR DASH

Determination
> "Passion costs me too much to bestow it on every trifle."
>
> THOMAS JEFFERSON

Attitude
> "I became an optimist when I discovered that I wasn't going to win any more games by being anything else."
>
> EARL WEAVER

Success
> "If your desires be endless, your cares and fears will be so too."
>
> THOMAS FULLER

Happiness
> "Love is a force more formidable than any other. It is invisible —it cannot be seen or measured; yet it is powerful enough to transform you in a moment, and offer you more joy than any material possession could."
>
> BARBARA DE ANGELIS

Part Four

HAPPINESS

"Happiness is placing your head on your pillow, knowing that you have taken steps to accomplish goals that make your life worth living."
—Eric J. Aronson

CHAPTER 22

Success is Not Happiness

During the first three sections of this book, I have provided a blueprint for success. If you become *determined*, develop the right *attitude* and employ the *success* traits of winners, you will eventually accomplish your mission in life. However, I think it is important to point out something very important – SUCCESS WILL NOT MAKE YOU HAPPY.

To many Americans, this statement may qualify as heresy. After all, haven't we been taught that success is the ultimate objective of life? In fact, one of the expressions I heard growing up was "Winning isn't everything, it's the *only* thing!"

Well, that simply isn't true. If it were true, then Elvis Presley might still be alive today. This man was a "winner" in almost every category you could imagine. He was good looking, talented, rich, famous and adored. However, he wasn't happy. As a result, he died trying to use drugs as an "escape" from his reality. This is despite the fact that his reality was the stuff of which most of our dreams are made of.

The same thing could be said for Marilyn Monroe, Jimi Hendrix, Janis Joplin, John Belushi, Chris Farley, River Phoenix – the list goes on and on. All of these people achieved enormous success but very little happiness. As a result, they died seeking happiness at the end of a bottle or a needle. And for some successful people, the end is much worse.

A striking example is the life and untimely death of Kurt Cobain, the lead singer of Nirvana. Nirvana's success story is the stuff of legends. In seemingly no time, the group built a local following, which turned into a national following, which transformed into a *global* following. The group sold millions of records in dozens of countries in just a few years.

At the center of this whirlwind of success was Kurt Cobain, who was widely acknowledged as the heart and soul of the group. By age 27, he had more money, fame and fortune than most of us could dream of having in ten lifetimes. Moreover, he had a wife and a young child. What more could anyone want, right?

There's only one more thing that anyone could want – happiness. At the height of the band's success in 1994, while on tour in Europe, Cobain overdosed on heroin. The tour was interrupted so that Cobain could enter a drug rehabilitation center. Unfortunately, within days, Cobain escaped from the center and returned to his home in Seattle.

On April 8, 1994, the music world was shocked when it learned that Cobain had died from a self-inflicted gunshot wound to the head. In his suicide note, he wrote: "I've tried everything within my power to appreciate it, and I do, God believe me I do, but it's not enough."

Now, I understand that there were complicated issues of mental health involved in Cobain's situation. However, the point still remains that success wasn't enough to make him happy. And this isn't an issue that's restricted to entertainers. I often meet men and women who have all the trappings of success, but who still aren't happy.

I'm not suggesting that there is anything wrong with success, or that success is the cause of unhappiness. Success is neutral in terms of bringing happiness into your life. It won't make you happy, nor will it make you unhappy. However, the problem is that many of us believe that success is the final piece in life's puzzle.

BE HAPPY NOW

We often say things like "When I finally get enough money to retire, then I'll be happy" or "When I meet the perfect mate, then I'll be happy." In other words, we allow our happiness to be contingent upon some goal or pursuit. Happiness is always something off in the distance – something to be enjoyed *later*. The problem with this approach is three-fold.

First of all, no one is guaranteed a "later." The only time we have is right now. Therefore, by delaying our happiness until *when*, we often end up denying our happiness altogether. Even in the most successful life, there are always goals and objectives for the future. Therefore, the time to be happy is *now* – not in the future.

The second problem with the "happiness when" philosophy is that we often don't recognize "when" when it arrives. In J. Martin Kohe's book, *Your Greatest Power*, he tells a story of a man who sold his belongings and went out in search of the touchstone. The touchstone was a small pebble with the power to turn any common metal into pure gold. The man had read in a book that the touchstone was on the shores of the Black Sea, lying among millions of identical-looking pebbles. However, the touchstone was different in that it was warm to the touch, while ordinary pebbles are cold.

Therefore, the man camped on the shore and began testing pebbles by hand. Each morning, the man would awaken and immediately start testing stones. To prevent himself from needlessly testing the same stones repeatedly, whenever he encountered an ordinary pebble, he would toss it into the sea. For three years, he went up and down the shore, picking up pebbles, feeling them for warmth and tossing them into the sea.

243

As you can imagine, this was tedious work that didn't bring the man much of a sense of accomplishment or pride. However, he persevered for the day *when* all of his effort would be worthwhile. On the magic day, he picked up a pebble and to his surprise, it was warm to the touch. However, he instinctively threw it into the sea before his brain had a chance to register that this was the touchstone he had been searching for all along.

This is what happens to many people who wait for "when" to be happy. They spend their whole lives throwing away experiences, looking for that one magic experience that will make everything worthwhile. They became so accustomed to thinking that happiness will arrive with the next experience that they miss it when it does.

> **"The trouble with opportunity is that it's always more recognizable going than coming."**
> **—Unknown**

The third problem with the "happiness when" strategy is that it leads to great disappointment if you never reach your "when." But, more importantly, it leads to devastating disappointment when you do.

This is most often illustrated with people who say, "*When* I become rich, then I'll be happy." For years, these people deny themselves any opportunity to be happy and instead, concentrate on getting rich. For reasons we've discussed earlier, this isn't the best strategy for getting rich. Nevertheless, sometimes these people actually achieve their dreams and become rich.

Then the reality hits them – money won't make them happy. I can't imagine too many things more devastating than to spend your dash in pursuit of a dream that was illusory. Perhaps this is why people say, "Be careful what you wish for because you just might get it."

HAPPINESS IS FREE

The "happiness when" philosophy is a recipe for disaster. Even worse, it causes unnecessary stress and turmoil. The truth of the matter is that happiness is available to each of us at *any* time with no strings attached. Happiness isn't material things or experiences. Happiness is the enjoyment of our thoughts and feelings. As a result, happiness is inside us and completely within our control.

> **"The happiest people are those who seem to have no particular reason for being happy except that they are so."**
> **—William Inge**

Remember, there is no way to happiness. Happiness is the way. Happiness is not a by-product of achievement but rather the by-product of our thoughts. Therefore, the key to happiness is to develop positive thought patterns.

No Regrets

I was recently sitting in a restaurant near two older gen-tlemen, and I couldn't help but overhearing part of their conversation. One turned to the other and asked, "If you had your life to live over again, what would you do differ-ently?" I waited anxiously as the second gentleman paused to collect his thoughts. Now, I know it's rude to eavesdrop, but I was fascinated to learn the answer to one of life's quintessential questions. Unfortunately, just then, laughter erupted at a nearby table and drowned out the gentleman's answer.

As you can imagine, I was very disappointed to miss out on this person's answer. In fact, I was tempted to walk over to their table and ask him to repeat it. Of course, I didn't. Instead, I pondered this question all the way back to the office and later that day, conducted a little research on this subject on the internet. In the process, I came across one study of 1,004 adults, age sixty-five and over, asking just this question. They answered as follows:

51 percent said they would have saved more money;

47 percent said they would have traveled more;

31 percent said they would have chosen a different career;

18 percent said they would have lived somewhere else;

As you can see, many people are living with regrets; and in some cases, major regrets. After all, one-third of these people spent a substantial portion of their waking hours engaged in the wrong career. Likewise, almost one-fifth of them spent their lives in the wrong city. In my view, this is nothing short of tragic.

I know that I've said this a thousand times before, but I will say it again, "Life is short!" And it's certainly too short to come to the end of it with major regrets. For this reason, I urge you to ask yourself this important question today, although you still have some time to affect the answer. If you had your life to live over, what would you do differently? And then, most importantly, do it.

If you think you should save more money, start saving. If you think you should travel more, start planning your next vacation. If you think you should work in a different field, then take some courses, read some books, and network with people in your dream field. And if you think you should live somewhere else, start making arrangements.

Now, you might be thinking that what I'm suggesting isn't that easy to do. Well, you're right. But it also isn't easy to live with regrets; living with what might have been. In fact, in comparison, anything is easier than living with the knowledge that your life could have been immeasurably better if only you'd only done something to change it.

"Accept the pain, cherish the joys, resolve the regrets; then can come the best of benedictions—'If I had my life to live over, I'd do it all the same.'"

Joan McIntosh

THOUGHTS FOR YOUR DASH

Determination

"You have to leave the city of your comfort and go into the wilderness of your intuition. What you'll discover will be wonderful. What you'll discover is yourself.

ALAN ALDA

Attitude

"I have no regrets because I know I did my best—all I could do."

MIDORI ITO

Success

"We must all suffer from one of two pains: the pain of discipline or the pain of regret. The difference is discipline weighs ounces while regret weighs tons."

JIM ROHN

Happiness

"Happiness is essentially a state of going somewhere, wholeheartedly, one-directionally, without regret or reservation."

WILLIAM H. SHELDON

CHAPTER 23

Don't Worry, Be Happy

Cicero said, "A happy life consists of tranquility of mind." He was right. It's very difficult to be happy while worrying about the economy, the latest terror alert or your Aunt Gertrude's gall bladder operation. One of the keys to experiencing joy is to eliminate worry from your life. And believe it or not, it's actually quite easy to do.

Michel de Montaigne once said, "My life has been full of terrible misfortunes, most of which never happened." I think that statement applies to each of us, regardless of our life experiences. For instance, I have experienced some really terrible things: abuse, the loss of my mother, and even incarceration. However, these pale in comparison to the horrors I have experienced in my mind through worry.

For instance, before going away to prison, I was absolutely *terrified*. Like everyone else, I had seen many of the prison movies. Therefore, in the months leading up to my incarceration, I mentally experienced every kind of horror imaginable. Fortunately, my actual experience in prison did not compare to the experience I had lived through in my imagination.

Being locked away from my friends and family and being surrounded by offenders (many of them violent offenders) wasn't fun, and I would never want to repeat the experience. However, *by far* the worst part of my incarceration occurred while I was still a free man as I worried about it.

I suspect that you have had similar experiences. You've worried about financial ruin that never occurred. Or you've worried about being diagnosed with a heart condition, only to discover that you had indigestion. Or perhaps you worried that your significant other was cheating with your best friend, only to discover they were planning a surprise birthday party for you.

> **"The anticipation of the punch is worse than the punch itself."**
> **—Eric J. Aronson**

In reality, very few catastrophes we worry about ever occur. And even when disaster strikes, it's almost always a lot less terrifying than we originally imagined. And this is really the key point – worry is nothing but the misuse of your imagination. Earlier in this book, we discussed in detail the benefits of thinking positively and visualizing your ideal future. Well, worry is the exact opposite of that process. Worry is thinking negatively and visualizing your perfect *nightmare*.

WORRY IS GIGO

As a result, worry not only kills any chance of joy in the present, but also prevents you from making the most of your dash. Remember, thoughts are things, and as such, they *create* our reality. In other words, you become what you think about. If you focus your mental power on all of the things that can go wrong, then your life will be filled with "wrong" experiences.

In fact, this principle is what gives power to Murphy's

Law: "Anything that can go wrong will go wrong and at the worst possible time." The interesting thing about Murphy's Law is that it doesn't seem to affect everyone. On the one hand, we all know people for whom Murphy's Law seems to have been written. On the other hand, we also know people whose lives are exactly the opposite. They are the people who always seem to be in the right place at the right time – the people with the "Midas touch."

In my view, the difference between these two groups of people is that the first set is ruled by worry while the second set is ruled by hope. Now, this isn't to say that "lucky" people don't have problems. Everyone has problems. However, "lucky" people tend to turn their problems into opportunities.

GET LUCKY

The good news is that luck is not some genetically pre-disposed trait, such as eye color or height. Luck is something that we all can acquire by the proper use of our minds. It simply requires that we recognize worry for what it is (the misuse of our imaginations) and banish it from our conscious-ness.

ACTION DEFEATS WORRY

This doesn't mean we should go into denial about our problems. In fact, denial is what usually causes most of our problems in the first place. We ignore the little problems in a marriage until the love is gone. We ignore the little prob-lems with our child's behavior until he or she is a monster. We ignore the little problems with our spending habits un-til we find ourselves under a mountain of debt.

By all means, deal with your problems. But don't con-fuse worrying about problems with actually *solving* them. They are not the same thing. In fact, when you start to solve your problems, your worry will disappear.

For instance, let's suppose you have been reading in the newspaper about the increasing cost of college and you realize that your current savings are woefully inadequate to pay for your child's college education. In this case, you have two choices: (1) to worry about the problem or (2) to solve the problem. As you know, worrying about the problem won't get you any closer to sending your kid to college. However, if you calculate the costs, formulate a savings plan and start putting aside money, your worries will disappear. This is because you've eliminated the need to worry about the problem because it's being solved.

LEARN ACCEPTANCE

You may be thinking that not all problems are within your control, and that is certainly true. However, even in those cases, worry isn't the best solution. Instead of practicing the dark art of worry, learn to practice acceptance. The ancient Greek philosopher Epictetus said, "There is only one way to happiness and that is to cease worrying about things which are beyond the power of our will."

Though he spoke those words almost 2,000 years ago, they are just as true today. When you are faced with possible disaster, simply accept the fact the worst possible outcome will occur. Immediately, you will feel a release of anxiety. There is incredible power in acceptance.

In a hurricane, the trees that survive the storm are those that sway and bend with the wind. However, the trees that stand firmly against the wind are eventually broken. The same thing applies to us when we face storms in life. We must learn to bend and move with the winds of adversity.

By being flexible, you can move on to more constructive thoughts, such as how you will handle the disaster, what strengths will you gain as a result and what you can learn from the situation. Remember, every problem carries within it the seed for your next success.

Couple your acceptance with the belief that you are strong enough to overcome the disaster, no matter what it may be. Acceptance becomes powerful because it removes the emphasis from the disaster and puts it back on you. Remember, what matters most is not what happens to you, but rather what you do about it.

Perhaps the best advice for learning acceptance can be found in the words of the Serenity Prayer:

"Lord, grant me the courage to change the things that I can change; the serenity to accept the things that I can not change; and the wisdom to know the difference."

LEARN TO LAUGH

It's often said that laughter is the best medicine. This is literally true. Glenville Kleiser says, "Good humor is a tonic for mind and body. It is the best antidote for anxiety and depression." In fact, a Northwestern University study demonstrated that laughing massages the heart, stimulates blood circulation and helps the lungs breathe easier. Interestingly, studies show that preschoolers laugh up to 450 times a day, while adults laugh an average of just 15 times a day. Perhaps this explains why so few preschoolers have migraines, ulcers and high blood pressure.

Humor can heighten any good experience, and can defuse tense situations. For instance, a police officer received a call to investigate a domestic disturbance. As she parked her patrol car in front of the house, a TV set flew through the second-story window. Obviously the situation inside the house had already gotten out of control.

As she approached the front door, she could hear loud voices arguing. When she knocked, an angry male voice screamed, "Who is it?" In a stroke of genius, she replied,

"TV repairman." The man broke into a fit of laughter and opened the door. Once inside, she was able to resolve the dispute easily.

We've all had experiences that were painful at the time, but we were able to look back later and laugh at them. In fact, some of our funniest stories come from troubling times – the day nothing would go right, or the big fight with our spouse or boss that resulted from a simple misunderstanding. In my view, the key is to learn to laugh at those situations while you are in them. After all, why wait to look back and laugh at a situation when you could be enjoying it right now?

Forgive and Remember

In my coaching practice, I find that one of the major issues for most of us is dealing with the need for forgiveness. Let's face it. We've all been hurt by others. Or, in other words, we've all suffered the slings and arrows of outrageous fortune. In some cases, these slings have been hurled by strangers and acquaintances. However, more often, we've been targeted by friends and loved ones. Obviously, these are the wounds that cut deepest and are the ones in greatest need of repair.

The simple truth is that resentment will do more to rob your DASH than any other mental condition. No matter how rich, famous, and successful you become, you'll never be truly happy so long as you're harboring resentment. Anger will eat away at any chance of experiencing joy in the present and even worse, it will steal your future. When you're angry, toxic levels of adrenaline and noradrenaline are released into your blood stream. Over time, these hormones can cause high blood pressure, heart attacks, strokes, and kidney problems.

The classic wisdom in this regard is the recommendation that you "forgive and forget" the wrongs of others. Well, as with many pieces of so-called wisdom, this is half right. You must certainly forgive those who have hurt you. However, the way to do so is not to forget their actions but rather to remember them and forgive them anyway.

For one thing, the advice to forget is impractical in most cases. Sure, it's easy to forget a minor trespass like the person who cuts you off in traffic or steals "your" parking space at the mall. These are minor matters that should be forgotten quickly. In fact, they shouldn't be given a second thought in the first place. However, how do you go about forgetting a major transgression, such as infidelity, sexual abuse, or some other violent crime? As the victim of sexual abuse, let me tell you that this isn't something that you can ever *completely* forget.

Therefore, instead of attempting the impossible, the key is to learn to give the experience a new, more powerful meaning for you. Besides, there are lessons to be learned from every situation in life. In fact, one of the most powerful lessons to learn is that you're a survivor and that you're bigger than anything that could possibly happen to you. Obviously, by going into denial about your past, you run the risk of not learning this most important of all of life's lessons.

Secondly, you shouldn't forget past hurts if you hope to protect yourself from being re-injured in the future. As the old expression goes, "Fool me once; shame on you. Fool me twice; shame on me." If you want your old wounds to heal, you can't have them constantly re-opened by your attackers. This requires that you remember what happened in the past and learn to avoid it in the future.

In some cases, avoiding future attacks is easy because you no longer have contact with your abuser. However, in some cases, the source of your past pain is a close friend or family member. For this reason, you may be forced to come into contact with this person from time to time. In those cases, it's extremely important to *remember* the past pain and look for ways to avoid it.

For example, let's suppose you have friends and family members who are dream killers. I know there are certainly those kinds of people in my family. In the past, I've excitedly shared my dreams with these people, only to have them ridicule me. After all, how was I, Mr. Least

Likely to Succeed, going to start a multimillion-dollar brokerage firm? Or how was I, Mr. Convicted Felon, going to start a national personal coaching practice?

The jeers and taunts of complete strangers can be painful. However, these same cries from your supposed "loved ones" can be outright devastating. Over time, I've learned to avoid this pain by simply not sharing my dreams with these people. Instead, we talk about other things—the kids, the weather, sports, etc. I'd suggest that you do the same thing with your critics. Likewise, if you know that a discussion about religion or politics is going to turn ugly with a certain family member, then avoid that topic before the insults start flying.

Of course, you can only do these things if you *remember* the past. And if you want to move to that all-important stage of forgiveness, then you must remember what you're forgiving the other person for in the first place. In fact, only by clearly remembering the source of your pain can you possibly come to grips with it and forgive the other person for their part in it.

For example, I only learned to forgive the dream killers in my life when I clearly looked back on the situation and began to see that their attacks were reactions to their own frustrations and broken dreams. When looked at from this standpoint, my anger turned to pity. I felt sorry that life had beaten their dreams out of them. In fact, I began to see that, in a strange way, they were actually trying to protect me from the frustration and disappointment they had experienced at some point in life.

I suspect that your tormentors and attackers have been the same way. Their unkind words and actions had little to do with you. They were in response to some deep-seated pain within themselves. Not knowing how to handle these feelings, they lashed out at you. When viewed in this light, their actions are certainly not justified but they are forgivable.

And even if they don't deserve to be forgiven, you deserve to forgive them. Remember, whenever you choose to remember your trespassers and forgive them anyway, you are doing yourself the biggest favor. You're freeing yourself to enjoy all the good things that this life has to offer. And by avoiding the toxic effects of anger, you're making sure that you're going to be around long enough to do just that. However, you can only enjoy the benefits of forgiveness so long as you forgive and remember.

"When you forgive, you in no way change the past—but you sure do change the future."

Bernard Meltzer

THOUGHTS FOR YOUR DASH

Determination
"The difference between the impossible and the
possible lies in a man's determination."
TOMMY LASORDA

Attitude
"I discovered I always have choices and sometimes
it's only a choice of attitude."
JUDITH M. KNOWLTON

Success
"Twenty years from now you will be more disappointed by the things that you didn't do than by
the ones you did do. So throw off the bowlines.
Sail away from the safe harbor. Catch the trade
winds in your sails. Explore. Dream. Discover."
MARK TWAIN

Happiness
"Happiness comes to those who are moving to-
ward something they want very much to happen.
And it almost always involves making someone
else happy."
EARL NIGHTINGALE

CHAPTER 24

Take a "Chill Pill"

Besides controlling anxiety, we must also learn to control anger. Anger is perhaps the most effective destroyer of happiness. It's awfully difficult to be happy when you are angry. Often times, we become angry when we are hurt or disappointed by the people in our lives. This is particularly true when the "culprit" is a parent, spouse, friend, teacher or co-worker. We can't control the actions of other people, but we can control our *reactions*.

THE NEGATIVE EFFECTS OF ANGER

The key thing to remember about anger is that even when it's justified, anger only hurts the person who is angry. After all, the last person who cut you off in traffic probably didn't give it a second thought. However, you may have let that incident ruin the better part of your morning. Allowing anyone to ruin even a minute of your day is just plain silly because you can *never* get that time back.

Even worse, anger is poison – literally and figuratively. The physiological changes that occur in your body as a result of anger are devastating. For instance, when you become angry, your body produces adrenaline and noradrenalin. These hormones stimulate the heart, dilate coronary vessels, constrict blood vessels in the intestines, and shut off digestion. Over time, this may lead to high blood pressure, headache, heart attack, stroke, and kidney problems. Confucius was 100 percent accurate when he said, "An angry person is always full of poison."

THE ONE MINUTE MADNESS

And these are just the physical effects of anger. Anger clouds judgment and causes people to do things they otherwise would not do. This is why we have crimes of passion, but not crimes of calm. Sadly, it only takes a second of anger to wipe out 30, 40 or even 50 years of a good living.

While in prison, I met several people who were victims of what I term the "one minute madness." These otherwise decent and law-abiding people became embroiled in one minute of anger that ruined their lives and the lives of others. Interestingly, when I talked with these men, most of them never foresaw the consequences of having a bad temper. They falsely believed that their rage would never get the best of them. Unfortunately, many of them learned too late that rage can get the best of *anyone*. The bottom line is that he who loses his temper usually loses.

DEALING WITH ANGER

Now, some people suggest that the way to deal with anger is to "get it off your chest." And surely, this is better than holding the poison inside. However, the problem is that we usually misdirect the anger at someone else. Therefore, in our efforts to get rid of our anger, we cause anger in others – usually our loved ones. Obviously, this isn't the best solution.

Of course, there are ways to get rid of your anger without taking it out on others. For instance, you could engage in strenuous physical activity. This is actually the best method because your body produces adrenal hormones to prepare you for physical activity in case you need to fight or flee. However, in the modern world, such a strategy may not always be practical.

For instance, let's suppose you get angry with your boss. What are you supposed to do – strip down to your shorts and start jogging around the conference room? I can't imagine this will improve your negotiating posture when you ask for your next raise. The truth is that many stressful situations don't allow an opportunity for immediate physical activity.

Many of us attempt to compensate by working out at the end of the day. The problem with this approach is that, by the time we get to exercise, the adrenaline is gone and the damage has been done.

AVOID ANGER

This is why I suggest you learn to avoid anger in the first place. This may sound impossible, but it's easier than you think. Remember, you are in control here. Believe it or not, the other person's words or actions are not what upset you. What upset you is *your* reaction to them. As Marcus Aurelius said almost two centuries ago:

"If you are distressed by anything external, the pain is not due to the thing itself; but to your estimate of it; and thus you have the power to revoke it at any moment."

There was a great Buddha who illustrated this principle. A man made an appointment to see the Buddha. The man decided that his objective would be to upset the Buddha, who was renowned for his serenity and sense of inner peace. Upon meeting the Buddha, the man immediately began slinging insults at the Buddha. He criticized the Buddha's appearance, surroundings and even the food and drink offered to him.

At one point, the great Buddha asked the man, "My friend, may I ask you a question?" The man, sensing that his insults were having an affect on the Buddha and expecting a stern rebuke, excitedly said, "Sure!" The Buddha then asked, "My friend, if you give me a gift and I refuse to accept it, who does the present belong to?" The man thought for a moment and then said, "I guess it would belong to me." The Buddha nodded and then asked, "So my friend, if you give me an insult and I refuse to accept it, who does it still belong to?"

No one can insult or hurt you without your permission. Have you ever heard the expression, "She let it roll off her like water from a duck's back?" We must all learn to be that duck. Even better, we should try to be the water.

Water has a great advantage over solids in that it has no set form. You can't break water. Nor can you crush or smash it. In fact, if you stomp in a puddle of water, what happens? The water gives in to the initial pressure and squirts out around the sides, usually wetting your shoes, socks and pant legs. In short, you can't win a fight with water because it simply yields to the force of your blows and comes out whole on the other end.

In the same way, people can't win a fight with you if you refuse their insults. Instead of becoming defensive and confrontational, simply accept the criticism. First, it may be valid, in which case you can learn something. Second, if it's invalid, then it will boomerang and strike the other person.

I once saw this in a comedy club. Someone decided the show wasn't good enough on its own and started heckling the comedian. However, instead of striking back in anger, the comedian simply ignored the heckler. Pretty soon, the audience turned on the heckler.

FORGIVE IMMEDIATELY

Now, I understand that this may sound a little too Zen for you. I'm a native New Yorker so it took a while for this concept to sink in for me too. In the meantime, I practiced the art of immediate forgiveness. In other words, as soon as someone made me angry (or rather I allowed myself to become angry), I would immediately say "I forgive you." Now, please note that I said this to myself. After all, you are taking your life into your own hands apologizing to a fellow New Yorker on the subway.

Give the Benefit of the Doubt

Once again, this isn't as difficult as it may seem, particularly when you try to see things from the other person's point of view. For instance, whenever someone cut me off in traffic, instead of displaying my "manual dexterity" out the window, I would simply imagine that they were on their way to the hospital to deliver a baby. Under those circumstances, their actions were completely justified. And besides, how do I know that it wasn't true? Therefore, I gave them the benefit of the doubt and freed myself from anger all at the same time. Not a bad deal all the way around.

Look For the Good

Another way to practice immediate forgiveness is to look for the good in every situation. For instance, let's suppose you are unfairly fired from your job. The normal reaction is to hate your boss and spend your energies concentrating on how you've been wronged. However, the better reaction would be to concentrate on the new opportunities now available to you.

This may sound like a "pie in the sky" concept, but think about it: Haven't the best things in your life resulted from being treated unfairly by others? You are married to the person you are now only because a previous boyfriend or girlfriend dumped you for "no good reason." You have the job you now have because someone refused to hire you at a previous company. You may even live in the house you live in now because someone refused to accept your offer at the first house you bid on.

Often, we look back on past "injustices" and become grateful. The trick is to learn to do it now and not years from now. Perhaps the best example of this concept involves the Argentine golfer Robert De Vincenzo.

After winning a tournament, De Vincenzo walked alone to his car when a woman approached him. She explained that her baby had an incurable disease. Almost without thinking, De Vincenzo endorsed his winner's check over to the woman and told her to "make some good days for the baby."

At the next tournament, a PGA official pulled De Vincenzo aside and told him that he had heard about what happened with the woman in the parking lot. The PGA official then told De Vincenzo that the woman was a con artist. De Vincenzo asked, "So you mean there is no sick, dying baby?" The PGA official nodded. De Vincenzo grinned and said, "That's the best news I've heard all week!"

Would that have been your first reaction? I'd like to think it would have been my first reaction but I'm not so sure. However, I am sure that it's the proper reaction. Either way, the money was gone. So isn't it better that there is one less sick baby in the world?

FORGIVE YOURSELF

Of course, while we are on the subject of forgiveness, don't forget to forgive the one person who needs it the most – you. If you are anything like me, then you have done some things in life you really regret. You may have regretted them almost immediately or it may have taken years to see the error of your ways. In either case, you must learn to forgive yourself.

A sense of guilt will kill any chance of experiencing happiness. In short, guilt is just another form of worry. Except with guilt, you put your negative focus on the past instead of the future. Either way, you aren't having much fun.

Also, it's very difficult to move forward while looking back. You can run much faster forward than you can run backward. Moreover, as you run your dash, you place yourself in great peril by continually looking backwards. You need to keep your attention on the hurdles in front of you, not the ones you've already stumbled over.

And, since you can't change the past, it doesn't make much sense to beat yourself up over it. Emerson had a wonderful philosophy about guilt:

"Finish each day and be done with it. You have done what you could; some blunders and absurdities have crept in. Forget them as soon as you can. Tomorrow is a new day; you shall begin it serenely and with too high a spirit to be encumbered with your old nonsense."

The key here is to remember that old expression "Don't cry over spilled milk." Think about it. What do you do when you spill a drink in the kitchen? Do you stand there and berate yourself for hours (or years) about how stupid and clumsy you are? Hopefully, the answer is "no." What you likely do is clean up the mess, fix a new drink and move on. This is what you should do with guilt as well. Find a way to repair the mess you've caused. Use your efforts to create a better result the second time – and move on.

"A retentive memory is a good thing, but the ability to forget is the true token of greatness."
—Elbert Hubbard

AVOID UNNECESSARY GUILT

Sometimes we assume we are to blame whenever someone is upset. If a roommate or significant other is in a bad mood, we assume they are mad at us and ask, "What did I do wrong?" Most often, they are upset with someone else. However, by assuming blame, we plant a very dangerous question into their subconscious mind. In essence, we ask their supercomputer to search its memory banks to discover what we did wrong. As with any good computer, it will continue searching until it finds an answer. As a result, we create conflict where it may not have existed.

In other cases, we unnecessarily accept blame when we make ourselves responsible for another's happiness. For instance, in a marriage, one spouse may assume responsibility for making the other spouse happy. Of course, we know that each person is responsible for his or her own happiness. However, by assuming responsibility for another person's happiness or well being, you set yourself up for failure in a situation over which you have no control. You also set yourself up for disappointment if the person doesn't appreciate all that you've done for them.

Now, should you be mindful of the feelings of others? Of course. However, their feelings are just that – their own. They "own" them. If a friend or loved one is hurting, then by all means, help them ease the pain, if possible. Just don't make yourself responsible for *their* healing. This is particularly true when people are upset because you didn't act in a way *they* thought you should act.

For instance, let's suppose your parents have always dreamed of you becoming a doctor. There is nothing wrong with that and be grateful that your parents have such high expectations of you. However, this is *their* dream for you. If your dream is to be an artist or a piano mover, then you shouldn't feel guilty for following your dream. After all, this is your life. And as far as we know, you only get one, so don't accept unnecessary blame because you can't achieve happiness or success living someone else's dream.

For instance, Ida and David wanted their son, Dwight, to go to college. However, Dwight decided to go to West Point instead. His parents were crushed by his decision. They wanted their son to be a doctor or lawyer, not a soldier. Fortunately, they held their tongues about their disappointment, but never withheld their applause. This was particularly true on the day their son, General Dwight D. Eisenhower, became President of the United States.

AVOID "STEALING" RESPONSIBILITY

Other times, we "steal" responsibility from others. This is common with parents, and I suspect that all parents are guilty of doing this to some extent. I know that I am. We sometimes tie our children's shoes, cut their meat or order for them at restaurants long after they are able to do these things for themselves.

Or perhaps our child has been assigned a science project at school. They enlist our "help" and before long, we are doing the entire project. Sure, we may end up earning an "A" on the project, but we earn an "F" as a parent. We have cheated our child out of the opportunity to learn and grow. I know how hard it is sit back and watch your beloved child struggle through a task. However, that struggle is necessary for your child.

One day, a young boy was watching a butterfly emerge from a small opening in its cocoon. The boy watched for several hours as it struggled to force its body through that little hole. Then it seemed to stop making any progress. It appeared as if it had gotten as far as it could and it could go no further. So the boy decided to help the butterfly by snipping off the remaining bit of the cocoon with a pair of scissors.

The butterfly then emerged easily. It had a swollen body and small, shriveled wings. The boy continued to catch the butterfly because he expected that, at any moment, the wings would expand and the body would contract in time. Neither happened! In fact, the butterfly spent the rest of its life crawling around with a swollen body and shriveled wings. It never was able to fly.

What the boy in his kindness and haste didn't understand was that the restricting cocoon and the struggle required for the butterfly to get through the tiny opening were necessary for the little butterfly's development. The butterfly's struggle for freedom forces fluid from its body to its wings, so that by the time it has achieved its freedom from the cocoon, it is able to fly.

The same is true for our children. They need struggles in their lives. Without them, they will never be as strong as they can be. Heaven help them if someone comes along and snips away their cocoons and by doing so, places them in a position for which they are not ready.

I understand that this is easier said than done and we will all fail from time to time in this regard but it's absolutely necessary that we struggle against this natural impulse to remove obstacles from our children's paths. We've all seen the result of "spoiled" children who are incapable as functioning as adults. As a parent, I suspect that it's very difficult to achieve any true happiness for yourself when your children are unhappy.

Put Your Trust In Others

There are so many myths swirling around the issue of success. And perhaps, the biggest one is the myth of the self-made man or woman. There is no such thing. And I say that as someone who has often been described as just that, a self-made man. Yet, the truth of the matter is that my success wasn't made by my efforts but rather the efforts of countless others. I've benefited tremendously from the assistance of others and so has anyone who has ever achieved anything great.

This is true even for people involved in activities that are normally regarded as solitary activities, such as painting, sculpting, and writing. Let's take, for instance, J. K. Rowling, the author of the enormously successful Harry Potter series of books and movies. If there was ever a self-made woman, she is it, right? Wrong! Sure, Rowling has the ability to create the stories all by herself but her success (and resulting riches) comes from the ability to get those books in the hands of her loyal readers. And this process requires the work of literally hundreds of people. Team Rowling consists of editors, literary agents, publicists, lawyers, distributors, promotional assistants, merchandising professions, and of course, the numerous people at her publishing company who take her manuscripts and turn them into finished books.

Now, you may not have aspirations of creating an international phenomenon, but even modest goals require teamwork. For instance, if your goal is to be the best parent you can be, you're going to need help. The old saying that it takes a village to raise a child is largely true. If you want to raise healthy, happy, and prosperous children, you're going to need a lot of help in the form of nurturing teachers who bring out the best in your child and adult family members who provide strong role models and a sense of identity. In fact, you'll even have to depend upon your child's peer group to an extent to encourage the right behaviors and discourage the wrong behaviors. In a very real sense, there's no such thing as a single parent. Nor is there such a thing as a sole practitioner, sole proprietor, or solo act, at least, not if they plan to be successful.

For many people, this is a difficult pill to swallow. After all, many people have been raised on phrases like, "If you want something done right, you have to do it yourself." As a result, they're reluctant to trust others to help them in the pursuit of their dreams. Sure, they *might* let others handle menial tasks for them, but they resist when it comes to letting others handle more important tasks. As a result, they end up spending too much of their time engaged in activities that could be better handled by others with more skill, experience, and inclination. Their unwillingness to trust others keeps them from making the kind of progress that they'd like to make in their journey.

The simple truth of the matter is that if you're going to go places in life, you must let others take the wheel from time to time. For example, in the past seventy-two hours, I've been on six different airplanes. As you can imagine, I didn't pilot a single one of these aircrafts. I simply sat back and left the flying to the pilots. I *trusted* that they had received the proper training, that the airplane had been properly maintained, and that someone had bothered to put enough fuel in the plane. I literally put my life in the hands of complete strangers.

When you think about it, this doesn't make much sense. After all, I didn't know these people. What if they somehow slipped through the cracks and were incompetent? Or what if they were just plain lazy? Or what if they were suicidal? How could I put my life completely in their hands? The answer is simple: Because I had somewhere that I wanted to go and I wanted to get there as quick as possible.

And you make a similar trade-off whenever you get behind the wheel of an automobile. You're trusting that the manufacturer built the car properly and that the steering wheel won't come off in your hands as you make a left turn. You're also trusting thousands of other drivers on the road to not run into you. This is a lot of trust to put into complete strangers, all of whom have different destinations than you do.

So if you can put trust in these complete strangers, then you can certainly trust the people who share your same sense of direction and purpose. In fact, if you're going to get anywhere at all in your DASH, you must begin to put your trust in others. Sure, from time to time, others will let you down, but you'll never get off the ground at all without their help and assistance in the first place.

"No one is useless in this world who lightens the burden of it for anyone else."

Charles Dickens

THOUGHTS FOR YOUR DASH

Determination
> "The people who get on in this world are the people who get up and look for the circumstances they want, and, if they can't find them, make them."
>> GEORGE BERNARD SHAW

Attitude
> "High expectations are the key to everything."
>> SAM WALTON

Success
> "You are never a loser until you quit trying."
>> TRINIDAD HUNT

Happiness
> "You may be deceived if you trust too much, but you will live in torment if you don't trust enough."
>> FRANK CANE

CHAPTER 25

Celebrate Thanksgiving Every Day

On the fourth Thursday of November, Americans celebrate a day of Thanksgiving. On this day, we gather with friends and loved ones to appreciate the blessings we enjoy. This is usually one of the happiest days of the year. My question is why do we only do this once a year? Why can't every day be Thanksgiving?

Of course, this doesn't mean that you have to cook a 20-lb. turkey, stuffing, gravy and cranberry sauce each day. However, it does mean that we should all make an effort to show more appreciation for our blessings.

This is contrary to human nature in some ways. For some reason, we naturally focus on what we lack as opposed to what we have. For instance, we usually only really appreciate good health when suffering from an illness or recovering from an illness. This is unfortunate because we miss out on a lot of the joy of appreciation this way.

Just think back to the last time you were sick. Now think of how happy you felt when you finally recovered. You could experience this exhilaration most days of the year if you simply took the time each day to appreciate the good health you usually enjoy.

MIX INSPIRATION AND APPRECIATION

For goal seekers like us, this is an especially difficult concept to grasp because so much of our attention is necessarily focused on our goals – things we don't yet have. However, appreciation and motivation are not mutually exclusive. We can be appreciative of what we have and still want to accomplish more. In fact, appreciation of our current circumstances can actually help us to reach new heights by showing us how much progress we've made so far.

One way to achieve an "attitude of gratitude" is to spend a few minutes at the beginning of each day reflecting on the things you *do* have in your life and how eagerly you would seek them if you didn't. For instance, as a father of four young children, I know firsthand the challenges of parenting. However, when I compare what my life would be like without my four children, I am grateful for every frustration and aggravation.

There's a story about a couple that gave a large donation to their church to honor the memory of their son who was killed in Vietnam. When the announcement was made, a woman whispered to her husband, "We should give the same amount in honor of our three sons." The husband turned to her and said, "Why? None of our sons were killed in the war." The wife replied, "That's exactly why we should do it!" Wow! What a change of perspective!

Often, I am saddened when I meet people who yearn for things only to obtain them and then not enjoy them. And we all know people like this. They work for years to finally be able to afford their dream house. They get the house and all they do is complain about how much the upkeep costs. People also do this with respect to jobs, businesses and even spouses. Actually, this is particularly true with spouses.

For years, we date various people looking for the "perfect" person. We finally meet him or her and everything is right with the world. In fact, things are so right that we decide we want to be with them for the rest of our lives. We then get married and, for a while, everything is great.

Then we start to focus on the shortcomings of our mates, and not the things that attracted us to them in the first place. To an extent, we are all guilty of behaving in this manner. Fortunately, once you recognize the problem, you can simply reform your thinking by making a mental list of all of the things you appreciate about your spouse and why you married him or her in the first place.

DON'T TRY TO KEEP UP WITH THE JONESES

Another thing we can do to maintain our attitude of gratitude is to refuse to compare ourselves with others. Often times, in our race to keep up with the Joneses, we fail to appreciate what we have. For instance, the neighbor next door buys a new car and now, for some reason, our car is no longer good enough despite the fact that we were perfectly happy with it last week. Envy and greed are destroyers of happiness.

This is beautifully illustrated in a Jewish parable. According to the parable, a greedy man and an envious man meet a king. The king says to them, "One of you may ask something of me and I will give it to him, provided I give twice as much to the other." As a result, neither man wanted to make the first request because they knew the other man would receive twice as much. Finally, the envious man agreed to make the first request and asked the king to pluck out one of his eyes.

The envious man was willing to turn his blessing into a nightmare in an effort to prevent his neighbor from being more blessed. Now, I don't imagine that any of us would go to such an extreme to stay ahead of our neighbor. On the other hand, I bet that if we each think about it hard enough, we'll probably find at least one instance when we've turned down a blessing to prevent someone from achieving a greater blessing.

This happens more than you'd imagine in the business world. Two people will walk away from a mutually profitable business deal because each thinks the other person is getting the "better" deal. In this case, each person chooses to receive *nothing* rather than allow the other person to get "more."

The key thing for us to remember is that we must learn to be happy with *enough* not excess. The ancient Greek philosopher Epicurus said, "Whoever does not regard what he has as most ample wealth is unhappy though he be master of the world." This is certainly true. You will never be happy regardless of how much you have if you don't think that it's enough.

COUNT THE COSTS

Likewise, you must learn to truly count up the "costs" of what you think you want out of life. And remember, the cost is not just the amount of money it will require to purchase it. There are other costs as well, such as how much time it will take away from your family and how much it will cost you in terms of stress and anxiety. In fact, these are the *real* costs of an item.

Therefore, before you go out and buy a new Mercedes Benz just because your neighbor bought one, count up the costs of the car. How many more hours are you going to have to spend away from your family to pay the car payment and insurance premium? How much less of a cushion are you going to have in case of a financial emergency? These are the real costs. Are they worth keeping up with the Joneses?

It's OK to Celebrate

Like most Americans, I spent much of yesterday evening watching the Super Bowl. Although I had no particular interest as a fan of either team, I found myself being excited for this year's Super Bowl Champions as they doused each other with champagne and held their trophy aloft in triumph. After all, it's not often that you get to witness such unbridled joy. And then it hit me...why not?

I'll admit that I like football as much as the next guy, but let's face it; it's only a game. No lives are saved. No enslaved people are set free. No cure is found for cancer, AIDS, or even athlete's foot. At the end of the game, the world is no better off for it. Yet, the winners hugged one another and cried tears of joy...and rightly so.

We could all learn a thing or two about the way these men approach the game of football and apply it to the way we approach the game of life. These men allow themselves to feel the exhilaration of victory. Do you? For instance, how did you react when you landed your last big account or finished a major project at work or moved into your first home or reached your 10th, 20th or 50th wedding anniversary? Did you raise your index finger into the sky and scream, "I'm #1"? No? Why not?

It's probably because you told yourself that your accomplishment was "no big deal". No big deal compared to what—winning a silly football game? You're accomplishments are a big deal, or at least, they should be. If you are as committed as I am to making the most of your DASH, your accomplishments are extremely important. They will change the course of history. So why not act like it?

Now, I'm not suggesting that every time you reach a goal at work, you should strip off your shirt and run around screaming, "Goooooaaaaaallllll!" However, I am suggesting that you allow yourself some form of celebration. Take your spouse to dinner. Invite your friends over for an informal party. Treat yourself to a day at a health spa or play golf at a really expensive course; the key is to reward yourself.

By establishing a reward, you will do two things. First, you will acknowledge to yourself that your accomplishments do matter. Second, you will train your subconscious mind to seek ways to achieve even more because it will know that there is an immediate payoff to success. Otherwise, you have taken the "joy of victory and the agony of defeat" and turned it into the "blah of victory and the agony of defeat."

And as important as it is to celebrate our own successes, we must be especially mindful to celebrate the success of our friends, colleagues, and loved ones. Whenever a professional sports team wins a championship, thousands of city residents turn out to meet their "conquering heroes" at the airport. Within a few days, the city organizes a ticker-tape parade and tens of thousands of people show up wearing T-shirts and exclaiming that their team is "#1." In fact, even the president of the United States gets into the act by inviting the victors to the White House.

However, when your colleague finally earned her master's degree after a dozen years of night classes, how did you react? Did you throw confetti at her? What about the time your friend finally bought his dream car? Did you meet him at the dealership wearing a T-shirt that read, "Larry's #1"? Or what about the time your child won the first grade spelling bee or the award for best basket weaving at summer camp? Did you celebrate that triumph by dancing in the streets or honking your car horn as you drove down the road?

Now, I understand that these examples may sound silly to you, but are they? Is a Super Bowl Championship any more important than your daughter mastering *Chopsticks* on the piano? I'm not so sure. And I am sure that it is far less important to your daughter. So why not give her just as much appreciation and adulation as you would give to a professional athlete whom you have never met and probably never will meet? Your colleagues, friends, and loved ones don't have millions of fans to cheer them on to victory, so they need *you* all the more.

"Celebrate the happiness that friends are always giving, make every day a holiday and celebrate just living!"

Amanda Bradley

THOUGHTS FOR YOUR DASH

Determination
> "The longer I live the more I am certain that the great difference between the great and the insignificant is energy—invincible determination—a purpose once fixed, and then death or victory."
>
> SIR THOMAS FOWELL BUXTON

Attitude
> "It is not the position, but the disposition."
>
> J. E. DINGER

Success
> "The will to conquer is the first condition of victory."
>
> FERDINAND FOCH

Happiness
> "A happy person is not a person in a certain set of circumstances, but rather a person with a certain set of attitudes."
>
> HUGH DOWNS

CHAPTER 26

Live In The Moment

Another big piece to the happiness puzzle is to learn to live in the moment. In a larger context, this means that we must learn to concentrate on *today*. Someone once said, "Yesterday is history and tomorrow is a mystery but today is a gift." Perhaps, that's why we call it the "present."

In fact, there is an ancient Sanskrit proverb that sums it up best:

> For yesterday is but a dream,
> And tomorrow is only a vision.
> But today, well lived,
> Makes every yesterday a dream of happiness
> And every tomorrow a vision of hope.
> Look well, therefore, to this day.

If, at the end of the day, you conclude that you spent the day being too stressed and too busy, you didn't accomplish anything and you didn't have any fun, then you have lost another precious day of life. This is a day that can never be replaced. It is gone forever. Instead, try to live the words of Henry Ward Beecher, who said: "No matter what looms ahead, if you can eat today, enjoy the sunlight today, mix good cheer with friends today, then enjoy it and bless God for it."

In fact, I would go so far as to say that we can't even be sure of *today*. After all, do you know what is going to happen between now and midnight? I don't! Therefore, we need to be concerned with living life *moment by moment*.

One way to do this is to take notice of the little things in life. It simply isn't possible to achieve big goals every day. For instance, no one can run a marathon everyday or climb Mount Everest or start a new business. These are all wonderful events but they require weeks, months or years of preparation. However, the question remains – how are you going to enjoy yourself in the meantime?

Therefore, the key is to find ways to make your daily life more enjoyable. For instance, let's suppose you like to spend time out in nature. As a result, you go to Yosemite for two weeks each year. However, should you only have two weeks each year of enjoyment? Why not drive to a local park and have a mini-picnic during your lunch hour. Remember, the point here is to incorporate enjoyment into your *daily* life since any day (including TODAY) may be your last.

How Are You Living Your Dash?

Last week, with great joy, I shared with you the news that a member of our DASH family had given birth to a new baby. Well, this week, I must share with you the tragic loss of a member of our family, Scott Hummel. In February, Scott was killed in a tragic automobile accident.

In my life, I have experienced some tremendous lows—sexual abuse, the loss of my mother at the age of thirteen, incarceration—and yet, I'm not sure that I have ever experienced a lower moment. Scott was one of the first employees of DASH Systems, LLC. He bought into the DASH dream when it was just that: a dream. At the time, we had just a few coaching clients, no book signings, no magazine features, no newspaper stories, and certainly, no national television exposure. Yet Scott was one of those unique people who had the ability to believe in the impossible.

He believed in this company when it was little more than letterhead and a catchy title. He believed in me when, to many people, I was nothing more than another ex-con with a get-rich-quick scheme. Each morning, he came into our lives with a smile on his face and a song in his heart. His enthusiasm, joy, kindness, and generosity were a living testament to what this company (and every company) should be all about.

The only solace that I can take in this tragedy is that the worth of a human life is not determined by its longevity. The worth of a human life is measured by what we do with that time we are allotted, no matter how long or short. It truly is the "DASH" between the years that makes the difference. And certainly, Scott Hummel made a difference. He made a difference in the lives of his family members, his friends, his community, and the members of the DASH family (both our employees and our clients).

In a very real sense, Scott epitomized the purpose behind this company and our mission. Our purpose is to help people to make the most of their DASH. And although we struggle to endure the pain of our loss, we are renewed in our commitment to our purpose—to his purpose. We are committed to helping others to find their true calling in life and make the most of their potential. We are committed to the principles that bring about success, abundance, love, and happiness. We are committed to treating others with respect, dignity, compassion, and concern.

And although we have by no means shed our last tears or asked our last, "Oh Lord, why?", we are more determined than ever to finish the work that Scott gave his heart and soul to help us start. Sadly, none of us has the power to add length to Scott's DASH, but with commitment, vigilance, and the grace of God, we can add some width and depth to his DASH. And that is precisely what we will do!

THOUGHTS FOR YOUR DASH

Determination

"With the power of conviction, there is no sacrifice."

PAT BENATAR

Attitude

"Determine what specific goal you want to achieve. Then dedicate yourself to its attainment with unswerving singleness of purpose, the trenchant zeal of a crusader."

PAUL J. MEYER

Success

"I would rather lose in a cause that will some day win, than win in a cause that will some day lose!"

WOODROW T. WILSON

Happiness

"When the heart grieves over what it has lost, the spirit rejoices over what it has left."

SUFI EPIGRAM

CHAPTER 27

Here's to Your Health

It's often said that if you have your health, you have *everything*. Well, that's not exactly true. After all, there are plenty of people in good health who lack many things necessary for happiness — loving family relationships, good friendships, challenging goals, financial stability, and a spiritual relationship with their Creator. However, happiness is virtually impossible without some measure of health. But many of us treat taking care of our health as a luxury consideration that we attend to only when everything else has already been taken care of.

For instance, if a big project deadline looms at work or family comes into town, the first things that goes is our diet and exercise program. We start grabbing "quick bites" and scrapping our workout plans with the promise that we will get "back on track" when things return to "normal."

MAKE YOUR HEALTH A PRIORITY

The sad truth is that intense work, family and social demands *are* normal. And as you start pursuing your mission, the demands in all areas become even more acute. This is why it's important to make good health an absolute *priority*. Instead of adopting the mindset that says, "I will eat well and exercise after my other obligations are satisfied," adopt the mindset that says, "I will eat well and exercise *while* satisfying my other obligations." After all, you can afford to lose a few dollars or a few hours of fun, but you only have one body, so take care of it.

Of course, this begs the question – "How do I take care of my body?" This may be *the* question in America today. As a society, we seem almost obsessed with fitness. Millions of us subscribe to fitness magazines, belong to fitness clubs and even shop at fitness stores. However, we are by no means a "fit" nation. In fact, we are amongst the world leaders in terms of obesity and all of its attendant health problems. As 17th century physician Thomas Moffett once said, "We are digging our graves with our teeth."

DEVELOP A PLAN

It's almost unimaginable that people who succeed so miraculously in most areas could fail so miserably when it comes to their health. I think the reason is our approach to the issue. We seldom strategize and plan our health programs the way we would if we were planning a business, a wedding or even a vacation. Earlier, we discussed in detail the dismal results you would achieve by not planning a journey to Disney World. Well, the same thing applies to a journey to a new body.

For instance, most people make a decision that they are going to "lose some weight." Well, that has as much power as planning a vacation *somewhere*. As you know, the first requirement to reaching any goal is to set a *specific* target. Therefore, it's important to specify how much weight and by when. It's also extremely useful to identity "why." You are much more likely to reach your goal if you have compelling reasons for success.

For instance, if you want to lose 15 pounds because you read in a magazine that your ideal is 15 pounds below where you are now, you probably aren't going to be very inspired to make the changes necessary to reach your goal. On the other hand, if you want to lose 50 pounds so you can play outside with your children and live long enough to see them graduate from college, then you will have a lot more motivation.

Of course, all the motivation in the world isn't going to help you if you don't have a good plan. And this is where most of us go terribly wrong. We get our diet plans from magazine articles, word of mouth, TV infomercials and basically anywhere but from the person who could give us the best advice – our personal physician.

Success in any area is not a "one size fits all" operation. It requires customized planning and this is particularly true when it comes to transforming your body. In short, you need one-on-one coaching from a trained professional. Therefore, the first step (after setting your goal) should be to make an appointment with your family doctor or a nutritionist to create your *personal* fitness plan.

Once you have a plan in place, then it's simply a matter of following your plan. Let me say that, from personal experience in this area (I once weighed almost 300 pounds myself), there is nothing more fulfilling than planning a fitness program and hitting your goal. The sense of accomplishment is almost indescribable.

GET PROPER REST

But don't think that proper diet and exercise are the only pieces to the health puzzle. You also need to get plenty of rest. And by "plenty of rest," I don't mean eight hours per day. You may need more or less sleep than most people. As a unique individual, give yourself the amount of rest that *you* require.

Also, please remember that "rest" means more than just sleep. It also means recreation and leisure. You must take some time to recharge your batteries. In his book, "The Seven Habits of Highly Effective People," Steven Covey illustrates this principle with the story of a lumberjack who is trying to cut down a large tree with a crosscut saw. Watching him struggle, a traveler suggests that he stop to sharpen his saw. The lumberjack replies that he would, but he's too busy cutting the tree down. Of course, what the lumberjack didn't realize is that he could have saved much more time by sharpening the saw.

We all tend to fall into this lumberjack's mindset from time to time. Often we say, "I'll take some time out for rest just as soon as I get this project completed." However, the truth is often just the opposite – "We will get this project completed just as soon as we take some time out for rest." Sometimes, the most productive thing you can do is to take a walk in the park, attend a concert, read a novel or work on your garden.

In fact, a wonderful thing to do for yourself is to spend a weekend at a health spa and resort. After all, you wouldn't drive your car for 50,000 miles without a tune-up so why would you drive your body 8,760 hours in a year without giving yourself a mental tune-up? And if you can't afford to spend a weekend at a fancy resort, then treat yourself to a "mental spa." Lock yourself in the bathroom for a couple of hours. Take a hot bath, listen to soothing music and just *relax*.

BREAK BAD HABITS

Of course, even with a wonderful health plan and proper rest, you're going to have trouble sustaining good health if you suffer from a dependency on drugs, alcohol or tobacco.

Over time, the effect of these substances will simply overpower the positive effects of a good diet, exercise and proper rest. Moreover, a dependence on any of these drugs will make it more difficult to maintain your health plan in the first place.

Now, I understand that it can be extremely difficult to deal with any of these dependencies but it is possible. For many years, my drug of choice was nicotine. One day, I decided that life was too precious to give up 10 or 15 years of it for the pleasure of paying $4 per pack to inhale stinky cigarettes. But even then, it wasn't easy to quit.

I was able to finally quit smoking by using one of the DASH Principles – I broke the project into bite-size pieces. At that time, I simply didn't have the will power to quit smoking for the rest of my life. So, one day, I decided to quit for just an hour. At the end of the first hour, I became curious about whether I could make it to lunch? After lunch, I thought, "Hey! That wasn't so bad. Let's try to make it until dinner." Once I made it to dinner, I thought, "Why not try to make it a whole day?"

Well, the day turned into a week and the week turned into a month and the month turned into a year. Now, please understand that there were many times when I had a "craving" for cigarettes. However, at that point, I wasn't unwilling to let all of my progress go to waste for one stinky cigarette.

Of course, this is by no means the only way to quit a bad health habit. In fact, there are dozens of programs to help you quit smoking, drinking or using drugs. If your health is important to you (and I know it is), then I *strongly* encourage to you to seek one out. I'm not saying that it will be easy but the benefits will be more than worth the trouble.

FOCUS ON OTHERS

Another great way to take care of yourself is to focus your attention on others. This is one of the primary reasons that I've stressed so heavily the concept of finding a mission in life. Once you become dedicated to a cause larger than yourself, you simply won't have time to get sick. One of the keys to a long (and happy) life is to always seek to give something of value to others.

"The surest way to happiness is to lose yourself in a cause greater than yourself."
—Unknown

This may sound like a trite expression but it's nonetheless true. In fact, one of the best examples of its truth involves an example from the physical world – The Dead Sea. As you may know, the Dead Sea derives its name from the fact that no plants or animals live in the Dead Sea. Obviously, this is highly unusual for a sea, which is usually teeming with all kinds of life.

So what makes the Dead Sea so different? The Dead Sea doesn't give of itself. Most seas flow into other waterways, which in turn, flow into other waterways. This creates a cycle of renewal and ultimately, life. However, the Dead Sea is merely an inlet. It takes all of the water it receives and merely holds it in a stagnant pool. As a result, it's merely a collection of dirty and extremely salty water.

This is what happens to a human being who stops giving and contributing. He becomes salty and all life within him soon dies. In fact, study after study has proven this to be true. People, who retire and become stagnant, die several years sooner than their counterparts who remain active in volunteer and charity organizations. A wise person once said, "We do not stop working because we are old, we grow old because we stop working."

Get Fed Up This Holiday Season!

Recently, I read that the average American gains seven pounds during the holiday season. This is in just over a month. If we were to eat like this all year, we would gain an average of *eighty-four* pounds in a year.

Fortunately for me, I read this statistic just before Thanksgiving. In years past, I would sit down at the dinner table on Thanksgiving and not get up until I had eaten everything but the tablecloth (I was saving that for dessert). Perhaps, that explains why three years ago, I was sixty pounds (or 8.5 holiday seasons) overweight. However, now, when I get "fed up," it's time to get up.

My question for you is "Are you fed up yet?" And I'm not just referring to food. Are you fed up with a poor relationship with your spouse or kids? Are you fed up with do-nothing friends? Are you fed up with spending day after day engaged in meaningless activities? And most importantly, are you fed up with you?

The most significant day of my life was the day I got "fed up" with my own mediocrity. I simply got tired of settling for less—less money, less love, less joy, and less meaning in my life. I got to the place of being broke, busted, and disgusted. This is a truly magical place. It's the place where you will discover what I discovered—there is more in you than you could ever know.

"If we all did the things we were capable of, we would literally astound ourselves."

Thomas Edison

By being "broke," I mean having just enough to get by. From a financial point of view, this is where your paycheck just covers your living expenses. Of course, you may be experiencing financial abundance right now but that doesn't mean you're not broke in some other area of your life. We don't just get broke in our bank accounts. Sometimes, we are broke in our relationships and careers and even, in our health. We have just enough peace, love, and understanding to make our relationships tolerable. Or we have just enough satisfaction, meaning, and joy in our careers to make them bearable. Or we have just enough energy and drive to make it through the day, but by 6:00 p.m., we are exhausted.

The problem with being broke is that it inevitably leads to being busted. For instance, if you are living from paycheck to paycheck, you run into trouble when an unexpected expense arises, such as a car repair. Likewise, if your relationship is broke, you may not have enough love and understanding when the challenging times arise (and they will). The same thing applies to your career and your health.

Sadly, many people live their whole lives in this situation. They struggle just to keep their heads above water. Then, when trouble comes, they find themselves submerged and spend months (or years), trying to break the surface. When they finally do, they go right back to treading water again. Unfortunately, for these people, they never reach the third plateau—being disgusted.

To make a major breakthrough in life, you must hit "rock bottom." And please keep in mind that rock bottom doesn't necessarily mean that you are living in a cardboard box under a freeway overpass. You can be living in a mansion and hit "rock bottom" (trust me on this one).

Rock bottom is simply the place where you are simply no longer willing to accept being broke in any area of your life. Once you reach this place, you will finally convince yourself that you deserve abundance in *every* area of your life and that you are willing to do *whatever* it takes to experience it. You are willing to forego immediate gratification to secure your financial future. You are willing to be more loving, kind, and generous with your family. You are willing to play the games at work, go back to school, or step out into a new line of work. You are willing to eat sensibly and exercise regularly for your health. In short, you are willing to do *anything* but be broke, busted, and disgusted.

As another year approaches, it's time for each of us to get "fed up" with the broken and busted areas of our lives. It's time for us to push back from the table of mediocrity and to start DASHing into our destiny.

"You and I have a rendezvous with destiny."

Ronald Reagan

THOUGHTS FOR YOUR DASH

Determination
> "I know the price of success: dedication, hard work, and an unremitting devotion to the things you want to see happen."
>
> FRANK LLOYD WRIGHT

Attitude
> "Our belief at the beginning of a doubtful under-taking is the one thing that assures the successful outcome of any venture."
>
> WILLIAM JAMES

Success
> "The conditions of conquest are always easy. We have but to toil awhile, endure awhile, believe always, and never turn back."
>
> MARCUS ANNAEUS SENECA

Happiness
> "Happiness is not pleasure, it is victory."
>
> ZIG ZIGLAR

CHAPTER 28

This is Just the Beginning

As you come to the end of this book, I want to reiterate that the DASH Principles work! They have worked miracles in my own life and in the lives of countless others. And like all principles, they not only work in 21st century America but they work anywhere and at any time. Throughout this book, I have given you example after example of people who used these principles to transform their lives, even though many lived half a world away and as many as 2,000 years ago.

Therefore, have faith; these principles will work for you as well. In fact, I suspect that if you've tried some of the ideas in this book, you are already seeing substantial changes in your own life. Perhaps, you have begun to take the first steps in your journey of fulfilling your ultimate destiny. Or perhaps, you have started the process of mending broken relationships with friends and family members. Or perhaps, you are just starting to feel more confidence and optimism about the rest of your dash.

Whatever your progress up to now, I want to strongly encourage you to keep it going! As we discussed earlier, motivation is not a permanent state of affairs. Of course, we often hear of people whose lives were changed "in an instant" but the truth is usually far less glamorous. Sure, we all have pivotal points in our lives and I truly hope that reading this book has been one of those points. However, change is seldom forged in those instances. True and lasting changing requires continual effort and application of winning principles.

In other words, you must replace mere inspiration with some actual perspiration. One form of perspiration will be in developing your *determination* and doing the in-depth planning necessary to accomplish your mission. And please realize that planning is a never-ending process. You can't simply make one roadmap to your destiny and follow it blindly. You will need to continually rethink your plan to account for bad weather, traffic, road construction and the many detours you will encounter along the way.

Another part of perspiration will be in developing the *attitude* of a winner. Once again, this attitude won't come overnight. It requires constant practice and reinforcement. In fact, even for someone like myself who has seen the enormous benefits of a proper attitude, I still catch myself engaged in "stinking thinking" from time to time. Of course, with time and some positive results, maintaining the proper attitude will be less difficult but it will still require diligence.

This is why I suggested that you set aside time *daily* for a mental check-up from the neck-up. After all, you wouldn't go days at a time without maintaining your physical body, would you? Could you imagine someone asking you when the last time you ate and replying, "I can't remember – it was either last Thursday or the previous Wednesday"? That would be absurd but no more absurd than neglecting to feed your mind on a daily basis.

Perhaps the biggest element of your perspiration will be in taking the steps of *success*. It may take weeks or months to break the habit of procrastination or to develop the friendships and alliances that are absolutely critical to your ultimate success. Likewise, you will continually struggle with your fears and overcoming adversity.

Once again, I'm not being negative but rather I want to prepare you for the road ahead so that you may be fortified for the battles to come. As any professional boxer knows, the most dangerous punch is not necessarily to hardest punch; it's the punch you *don't* see coming.

This is one reason that I've been so brutally honest with you in this book. I haven't promised that your dash will be easy. Nor have I promised that you will never encounter disappointment, hurt and pain. You will encounter all of these things. They are part of the human condition. Furthermore, I have gone out of my way to destroy the myth that success equals happiness. In my view, this is the ultimate punch that people don't see coming at them and the results are particularly devastating.

The DASH System isn't your guide to an easy life but it is your guide to a better life. Although the DASH Principles will not remove all of the pain and disappointment from your dash, they will make your dash a lot less painful and disappointing than most. Moreover, you will experience a sense of joy and abundance that is only felt when you have made your dash all it could be.

It's Not How Hard You Fall; It's How High You Bounce

Every day, we pick up the newspaper and it seems as if the world is simply full of disaster and turmoil. There is war and senseless violence in the Middle East. Hurricanes and tropical storms continue to ravage the Caribbean and parts of the southern United States. With all the trouble in our world today, we can't help but to have questions like "What's next?" and "Who's next?"

Well, I hate to be the bearer of bad news, but to answer your question you're *next*. The simple truth of the matter is that we all will face our share of disasters during the course of our DASHes. We will have marital problems, financial difficulties, legal troubles, family squabbles... you name it. As Longfellow once wrote, "Into each life a little rain must fall."

For this reason, the most important factor in the success of your DASH is not whether you face adversity (you will) but rather how well you deal with it. For some people, when trouble strikes, the focus becomes simply surviving on the situation. However, the real winners in life not only look for a way to survive tragedy but to thrive in the face of it. Thomas Edison was a great example of a person with just this kind of mentality.

In *The Electric Thomas Edison*, Edison's son tells the following story about his father:

> "I especially recall a freezing December night in
> 1914 at a time when still unfruitful experiments on
> the alkaline storage battery to which my father had
> devoted ten years had put him on a financial
> tightrope. On that cold December evening, the cry
> of 'fire!' echoed through the plant.... When I could

not find my father, I became concerned. Was he safe? And with all the assets going up in smoke, even if he was safe, would his spirit be completely broken? He was sixty-seven years old, and it seemed to me as though it was no age for dad to start over again.

At 5:30 a.m. the next morning, the fire barely under control, dad called all of his employees together and announced, 'We're rebuilding!' ...Later on, he explained to me, 'You can always make capital out of disaster. We just cleared out a bunch of old rubbish. We'll build bigger and better on these ruins.' And we did; we built bigger and we built better."

We would all do well to learn to build bigger and better on the ruins in our lives instead of simply trying to recapture what was lost. Therefore, the next time you face a challenge, ask yourself, "How can I not only survive but thrive in this situation?" That's exactly the question I asked when I was sent to prison. I knew I had three years to spend there and I could either serve the time or let the time serve me. I chose the latter. I made it my mission to walk out of prison a much better person than when I walked in. That's why I read every book I could get my hands on. That's why I quit smoking, gambling, and lost thirty-seven pounds. That's why I started focusing my effort on finding a way to help others achieve the success they wanted out of life.

And although I certainly hope that you never have to experience the troubles I've faced in life, I want to encourage you to take the same approach when challenges come your way. As someone once said, "When trouble moves in, make it pay the rent." You make trouble pay the rent by improving your circumstances with every setback. If you are fired or laid off from your job, take the opportunity to look for an even better job, go back to school, or start your own business. If your landlord throws you out of your apartment, take the opportunity to purchase your own home. If your boyfriend, girlfriend, or significant other dumps you, take the opportunity to find an even better looking, smarter, funnier, and more loving companion.

Remember, it's not how hard you fall in life; it's how high you bounce.

"Be courageous. I have seen many depressions in business. Always America has emerged from these stronger and more prosperous. Be brave as your fathers before you. Have faith! Go forward!"

Thomas Edison

THOUGHTS FOR YOUR DASH

Determination
"As long as you're going to think anyway, think big."
DONALD TRUMP

Attitude
"The size of your success is determined by the size
of your belief. Think little goals and expect little
achievements. Think big goals and win big success."
DAVID J. SCHWARTZ

Success
"To finish first, you must first finish."
RICK MEARS

Happiness
"When we travel life's roads with those we love,
the point of destination is always secondary to the
quality of the journey."
MARY PRINCE

EPILOGUE

While books, audio programs, video programs, and seminars all have their place in your personal development quest, the single greatest tool to help you create an extraordinary dash is personal coaching. Let's face it. Sometimes we are simply too close to a situation to be able to analyze it properly. At those times, we need someone who can view the situation from another perspective.

A BIRD'S EYE VIEW

This is a concept that professional football coaches understand and use to their advantage. In professional football, the head coach stands on the sidelines and monitors the progress of the game, making adjustments and giving instructions. Nevertheless, he understands that from his vantage point, he only sees a small part of everything that is unfolding during the game. As a result, he has a team of coaches who sit high above the field and provide input from their vantage point. This input allows the head coach to make better decisions.

Can you think of a time in your life when you could have

used input from someone with a different perspective on the situation? I can think of *several* times when I could have benefited from a "bird's-eye view." In fact, some of my greatest setbacks occurred because I made decisions without realizing the full impact of those decisions. A third-party perspective can fill in the big picture.

GETTING THE RIGHT FEEDBACK

Of course, most of us already know the benefit of getting feedback from others. We do it every day. When we have a big decision to make, we usually seek out the advice of our friends and family. However, as you've probably experienced, this doesn't always result in getting the best advice. Sometimes we get good advice and sometimes we don't. This isn't because our friends and family don't love us or want the best for us but it's simply because they don't always have the knowledge or experience to provide the best advice. There is an old expression that I'd like you to keep in mind: "The fool asks the wise for advice, but the wise ask the experienced."

For instance, when I initially became interested in golf, the first thing I did was sign up for lessons with the local golf pro. Sure I had many friends who were golfers but I was looking for instruction from an expert. My expert taught me how to properly grip the club, and how to stand, pull the club back, shift my weight, swing and follow through.

Of course, all of this information was available in books and videocassettes. However, what was not available in books and videocassettes was the one-on-one feedback. A book can't say, "Eric, don't bring your head up so soon" or "Eric, widen your stance about an inch." This individual feedback was necessary for me to develop the right habits.

The most successful athletes in the world understand this principle. Perhaps that's why they all have personal coaches. Tiger Woods has a coach. Venus Williams has a coach.

Tara Lipinsky has a coach. Isn't your dash through eternity at least as important as a sporting event?

At Dash Systems LLC, we are committed to helping you make your dash as meaningful as possible. In fact, this is what gives our dash meaning. We have assembled some of the top coaches in the field of personal development. These highly successful individuals not only teach the DASH Principles, they also live them to enhance their own lives. We are passionate about our work and we know we can make a difference. For that reason, we are offering an introductory coaching session for FREE. Simply email us at info@dashlive.com to speak with one of our coaches. I can assure you that it will definitely make a difference in your dash

In that vein, I sincerely hope that this isn't the end of our relationship, but merely just the beginning. Your dash deserves every advantage you can give it, so why not avail yourself of a tool used by almost all peak performers? At Dash Systems, LLC, there is nothing more important than your dream, and we are dedicated to bringing all our love, compassion and wisdom to bear in that pursuit.

Finally, I would like to say, "Thank you!" It is my pleasure to share these principles that have made such a huge difference in my life. One day, I look forward to hearing your stories of triumph. Please feel free to keep in touch through our website at www.dashlive.com. There, you will find helpful tips and hints on how to make the most of your dash. Once again, thank you and God Bless.